Stitches, Patterns and Projects for Knitting

Also by Wanda Bonando

Stitches, Patterns and Projects for Crocheting

Stitches, Patterns and Projects for Needlecraft (with Marinella Nava)

STITCHES, PATTERNS AND PROJECTS FOR KNITTING

Originally published in Italian in 1979 by Arnoldo Mondadori Editore S.p.A., Milan under the title *Guida alla Maglia*

Copyright © 1979 Arnoldo Mondadori Editore S.p.A., Milan English translation copyright © 1984 Arnoldo Mondadori Editore S.p.A., Milan

Translated by Sylvia Mulcahy

FIRST U.S. EDITION

Library of Congress Cataloging in Publication Data

Bonando, Wanda.
    Stitches, patterns and projects for knitting.
    (Harper colophon books; CN 1094)
    Translation of: Guida alla maglia.
    Includes index.
    1. Knitting. I. Title.
TT820.B68513 1984   746.43'2   83-48328
ISBN 0-06-091094-1 (pbk.)

84 85 86 10 9 8 7 6 5 4 3 2 1

Diagrams: Studio M.P. Team, Milan
Color photographs: Roberto Circià
Photographs on pages 159 and 178: Studio Ranzini, Milan

Printed in Italy by Arnoldo Mondadori Editore, Verona

Contents

7 *Introductory Notes*

15 **Beginning: knit and purl**

16 CASTING ON, BASIC STITCHES AND SPECIAL STITCHES
17 Casting on
23 Basic stitches
25 Special stitches

28 INCREASING, DECREASING AND FINISHING
28 Increasing and decreasing
34 Selvedges and borders
37 Hems and corners
40 Buttonholes and pockets
43 Neck openings, necklines and sleeve fittings
48 Pleats and tucks
50 Binding off, repairing, trimming, blocking and finishing

59 **Imagination and creativity: decorative stitches**

60 BACKGROUND STITCHES

96 OPENWORK STITCHES AND JACQUARD DESIGNS
96 Openwork stitches
131 Jacquard designs

135 **Putting it all into practice: standard patterns**

136 KNITTED THINGS TO WEAR
136 Patterns for women
169 Patterns for men
178 Patterns for children
195 Patterns for babies and toddlers

216 KNITTED ACCESSORIES

228 KNITTING FOR THE HOME

244 USEFUL AND FUN THINGS TO KNIT WITH SCRAPS

251 *Index*

INTRODUCTORY NOTES

Carding, spinning and weaving, operations in the working of wool that are as ancient as history itself, have been so skillfully perfected that we now take for granted one of the most flourishing manufacturing industries in the world today. Through the centuries, right up to the beginning of the 16th century, Ancient Greece and Rome, Medieval Europe, France and Italy led the way in the production and marketing of beautiful fabrics which were greatly sought after and highly prized. Britain's reputation for fine woolen cloth was to come a little later, perhaps because most of its raw wool had hitherto been exported to Florence for manufacture into exquisite articles. But it was the Industrial Revolution which was to change the situation. Mechanization soon came to the woolen cloth industry and the introduction of spinning machines and mechanical looms gave the monopoly of the trade to those countries in the forefront of the movement.

While exact dates are not available, it would seem that the technique of producing knitted fabrics is just about as old as that of producing woven materials.

It is only possible to hazard a guess as to what led up to the production of fabrics by means of a series of stitches rather than by the intermingling of warp and weft on a loom. It seems likely that the new technique was invented to meet the need for a more elastic material which could be used in conjunction with the rough, rather stiff fabrics of those far off times and which would adapt itself better to the shape of the human body. The technique would still have been based on a loom, probably working on a net foundation, rather like a fisherman's net, in an attempt to obtain a finer stitch.

This would seem to be confirmed by the earliest finds it has been possible to examine – the most ancient that have so far come to light – fragments of cloth, hosiery and head-coverings which had belonged to the Coptic peoples. Discoveries of a more recent date, found in Egypt and also in several Viking tombs in northern Scandinavia, have made it possible to be more precise as to the various stages of the work, which was already fairly technically advanced. These fabrics – known as *sprang* – were worked with a sewing needle on a vertical weft mounted on a wooden loom and secured by means of knots. A feature of the resulting fabric, which consisted of small, closely worked stitches, was its remarkable elasticity, obtained by weaving a woolen thread in and out of the foundation weft and fastening each stitch with a small knot.

A second system saw the introduction of knitting needles. These were made of wood, one of them being inserted between the stitches, carrying the yarn around in order to anchor each stitch as the work proceeded. In this case, the basic weft or ground threads consisted of threads woven singly, one at a time, on to a loom, the work starting from the center and moving up and down. The stitches of the resulting fabric were thus more regular and symmetrical than before.

While this technique was being developed in Egypt and Scandinavia (between 1500–1000 B.C.), a remarkably similar method was being developed in faraway Peru. It was being used there to produce a foundation fabric for a type of crude but colorful embroidery of a very distinctive and lively character.

The next step forward was in the development of a knitting loom which was the forerunner of the machines used today in making knitted fabrics. It was normally a square apparatus with a series of small hooks all the way around over which the stitches were worked with a single thread. Once again, it was in North Africa that this new method evolved and early examples of the work reached us from Arabia and Egypt. Fragments of material found in the ruins of Fustat – where Cairo now stands – dating back to the 9th–7th centuries B.C. are undoubtedly the result of this new technique. It is interesting to note that a type of crochet hook must have been used to carry the thread over the hooks and that this is a characteristic feature of several types of craft-work still being executed, apart from crochet, which have roots in the old traditional methods.

A number of woolen head-coverings were found in Egypt and North Africa, dating back to the 1st century B.C. An early Christian sect learned the method of knitting on a hooked loom from nomads in the Egyptian desert, which gives some indication of how long the system had already survived.

Until comparatively recently, most knitting was worked in one color of wool only, very often in natural unbleached wool. This applied everywhere except in Peru, as already mentioned. However, examples of knitting in several colors began to reach Europe from the Middle East and this was to introduce a totally new approach to the craft. Spain was the first country we know to have allowed the work to blossom from being purely useful into a glorious art form. A magnificent altar glove, such as would have been worn by a bishop, has survived from the 11th century as evidence of the fine use of color. The new technique soon spread to France and Portugal, developing until the fabric became very much as we know it today.

The work was now being done less on a hooked loom and more on a single knitting needle upon which all the stitches were worked. This needle was mounted on a support to enable it to be attached to the worker's belt or to be tucked under the arm. Various types of accessories were adopted for this purpose, including wooden rods, reeds bound together (these were used mostly by farm workers and fisher-folk) or small cloth or leather bags stuffed with straw, horsehair, wood shavings or dried grasses. In Yorkshire, for example, the support for the knitting needle was made with one end flat and curved over so that it could be slipped through the belt or under the arm, thus giving the user freedom to move about, talk to friends and neighbors and carry on with the work even in places not usually associated with such a domestic task. And there was a particular reason for this. Knitting was primarily a masculine occupation to fill in free time in the normal working day of sailors and fishermen, farmers and shepherds. Their speciality was knitted caps but they also made stockings and other garments for themselves and their families. The women concentrated more on the work which had, by tradition, become an important home industry, that of carding and spinning the wool and then weaving it into cloth.

The first knitting guilds were formed in the late Middle Ages, the most outstanding in Paris and Florence. These guilds, which were organized on very strict lines, became highly professional and the technique of knitting improved to such an extent that it became one of the leading artisan crafts.

Trainees were apprenticed for three years to a master craftsman in whose workshop they learned the basic elements of the work. They were then sent abroad for a further three years, to be taught the finer points. On their return, they were obliged to submit to a stiff examination by the master craftsman to whom they were apprenticed and for this they were expected to make a carpet or wall-hanging in twenty or thirty different colors, a shirt, an elaborate cap and a pair of stockings.

Severe penalties were inflicted upon anyone who violated the guild's code of rules, the main purpose of which was to protect the secrets of the profession.

The Florentine knitting industry of the 16th and 17th centuries produced fabrics which were both warm and delightfully soft. These beautiful materials were greatly admired in all the courts throughout Europe and the supremacy of the Parisian guilds was seriously threatened. However the French, with their great experience and tradition of design and workmanship, were soon producing fine hosiery and woolen garments which rivalled even the most delicate laces.

Knitting skills and techniques continued to develop and improve in a number of countries as demand for the fabrics increased. The work became particularly popular in Germany, where it acquired a character of its own with the use of a great deal of ribbing combined with knot-like stitches to produce a heavier fabric. Similar patterns were also emerging in the Aran Isles in Galway Bay off the coast of north-west Ireland. There the fisher-folk, using the raw locally produced wool, started a tradition in heavy knitwear which continues to this day.

At the same time, designs were being produced in Germany, Britain and Holland in which the stitches normally used in hosiery making were reversed. This gave a rich, textured fabric and was mainly used in the making of elaborate garments for royalty and the aristocracy. King Charles I thought so highly of a particular knitted bodice that he wore it to the scaffold on the day of his public execution so that it might be recorded for posterity in the inevitable paintings of the event. History also tells us that London was covered in about six inches of snow on that day, January 30, 1649, and the King was anxious to keep warm so that he would not shiver in the cold and be thought a coward.

The delicate floral and bird designs, which were typical of work being produced in Holland, also became very much sought after and in fact the King of Denmark, enchanted by a pair of knitted breeches given to him as a gift, had a request sent to Amsterdam for Dutch knitters to come to his country so that they might teach their skills to his own subjects.

The lowly origins of this craft, which were based entirely on hand-work, were to be completely over-shadowed, if not obliterated, by the commercial mass-production of knit-wear that was to emerge with the advent of the Industrial Revolution.

As far back as 1589, during the reign of Queen Elizabeth I, a church diplomat named William Lee of Cam-bridge, who was born in Notting-hamshire, had already designed and completed the very first knitting loom. Its specific purpose was the making of hosiery and the principles upon which it was based were partly derived from the ancient Arab tech-niques. Although ingeniously de-signed, Lee's machine was really simple in conception; the stockings were worked on a flatbed and shaped by means of two rows of hooks, one fixed and the other mobile, while the yarn was carried by a system of weights and springs.

Because of the violent opposition aroused by these methods among hand-knitters, and finding no support in his own country, Lee went to France where he sought protection in the Court of King Henry IV. Even there, life was not easy for him and it was not until late in the 18th century, long after his death in 1610, that Lee's machine was finally estab-lished. The result was that hand-knitting was almost totally sup-planted and the foundations of to-day's flourishing, worldwide industry were laid. Modern knitting machines are still based on the same principles as the machine invented by Lee nearly four hundred years ago.

At the end of Elizabeth I's reign, hand-knitting had almost completely disappeared, not only in Britain but in the whole of Europe. Only in a few areas, such as Yorkshire, was a living still to be earned by hand-knitters right up to the 19th century. In this northern county of England, the tra-ditional four needles were used to make socks and stockings, the most celebrated examples of the work being the long stockings which were worn inside the high boots of the Cavaliers. Elsewhere, the craft had returned to its humble beginnings as a purely domestic skill. With the spread of colonization and the emigration of whole families to the New World, the craft adapted to local conditions – available materials were not always the same as those that had been used at home – and developed new characteristics.

Our own century has seen a great rediscovery not only of the practicali-ty and economy of knitting clothes for oneself and one's family but also a reawakening to the fascination of working in such a flexible medium in which the only limits are those of one's own creative imagination. The need for individual creativity has probably never been greater than now, when there is such a desire to escape from the impersonal uni-formity of present-day fashion.

The present range of wools and man-made fibers, in all thicknesses and textures, offers such a wealth of stimulating possibilities that it is sometimes hard to decide which yarn to use for a garment.

Equipment for hand-knitting

For a beginner who wants to learn to knit, the only essential equipment is a pair of knitting needles. However, there are a few other items which, although not essential, will facilitate the work and save time.

The most usual type of knitting needles have a point at one end and a knob at the other to prevent the stitches from falling off. They vary in diameter, according to the thickness of yarn to be used. American needles range in size from Number 0 to Number 15, with the larger needles represented by the higher numbers and the very fine needles having the lower numbers. When knitting with finer yarns for such things as lacy jumpers, evening tops or baby clothes, low numbered needles are used while the opposite is the case when using thicker wools for more casual clothes.

There are also double pointed needles which are used in the round for neck and cuff ribbing and to make socks, gloves, turtle necks and other items that are more satisfactory without a seam. These 'sock-needles' are usually sold in sets of four – although in some countries they may be found in sets of five. In many patterns where the neck or wrist stitches have to be picked up to work the collar and cuffs, the pattern will indicate that four needles are to be used. Shorter double-pointed knitting needles can also be obtained, sold singly; these are to facilitate cabling, when a few stitches have to be carried in front or behind the work from time to time.

Also to be found in yarn shops or in the knitting departments of large

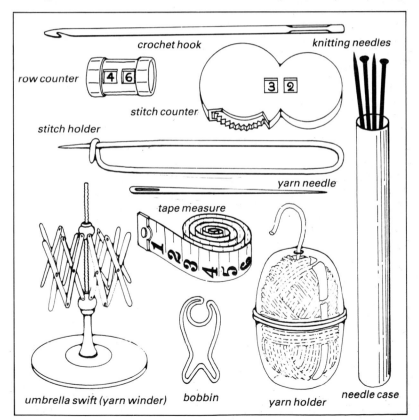

crochet hook

knitting needles

row counter

stitch counter

stitch holder

yarn needle

tape measure

umbrella swift (yarn winder) bobbin yarn holder needle case

stores are circular needles. These are made up of two double-pointed knitting needles joined together by a length of plastic wire and are used in the same way as sets of four needles except that they are for large garments, such as skirts, worked in the round.

When selecting the appropriate size of needles, the deciding factor is the weight of the yarn to be used. Weight refers to the thickness of the yarn. When using knitting worsted for instance, the usual size needle to use would be number 7, 8 or 9, but a great deal depends upon the individual tension at which the knitter works. If the tendency is to knit rather tightly then larger needles should be used while, conversely, if the work is inclined to be loose, then smaller needles are required. Normally a size one way or the other is adequate for the adjustment.

Knitting needles are made of various materials, the most common these days being aluminum or plastic. There are also steel and wooden needles. Every knitter will develop their own preference of needle type with experience.

It is also a good idea to have two or three crochet hooks available in various sizes for picking up dropped stitches (this applies especially to beginners) and in working some types of stitch. They are particularly useful, of course, for finishing off the edges of collars, cuffs and jackets as this gives a very 'professional' look to garments.

Other gadgets which are handy but by no means essential include stitchcounters and rowcounters, which also sometimes contain a short tape measure. These may be slipped on to one of the needles (only in the case of two needled knitting, of course). When four needles are being used, the counters can be kept nearby or attached by a thread to a buttonhole or worn as a pendant by the knitter. They are manually turned to record the number of rows worked or stitches increased or decreased and save a great deal of time – and annoyance – in repeatedly counting rows or stitches.

Another useful accessory is a stitchholder. This is rather like a large safety pin onto which stitches which have to be left unworked can be slipped while the work is continued on the remaining stitches. The advantage of this is that the stitches are securely held whereas if they were left on a spare needle they would be inclined to slip off.

Point protectors made of rubber or plastic prevent stitches from accidentally slipping off the needles between work sessions. There are several sizes to accommodate fine as well as bulky needles. If you do not have point protectors, push stitches back from the needle tips before you put your knitting away.

Another accessory which is useful when yarn is purchased in skeins is an umbrella swift (yarn winder) which may be made of wood or metal (see illustration on page 11). To protect knitting needles from getting rusty (this applies only to steel needles, of course) and to protect the points, a tubular holder or a folder in which each size has a separate pocket is recommended – the latter can easily be made at home from a piece of strong cloth and tied with tape.

While working, a yarn holder helps to keep the yarn clean and prevents it from falling on the floor. The holder is simply a container with a hole in the top through which the yarn passes; the ball of yarn turns freely inside the holder.

When working in several colors,

such as Fair Isle or jacquard designs, it is usual to wind the colors onto bobbins in order to avoid tangling the yarn as the change-overs are made at the back of the work.

Two essential items for almost any type of work are a tape measure and a yarn needle. The most practical tape measure is the small, retractable type which takes up little room in a knitting bag (another useful accessory, to contain all the necessary equipment). The yarn needle is similar to an ordinary sewing needle but with a fairly large eye to allow the yarn – which should be of a type suitable to the work in hand – to pass through easily. The needle is used to sew the pieces of a garment together, to embroider over knitting or to edge with blanket-stitching.

Glossary of basic terms

In addition to the more technical terms used in knitting, some of the words used in the text which might not be immediately understood are listed here for ease of reference, with relevant abbreviations where appropriate. Further abbreviations will be found in the next chapter, in the explanations on basic stitches.

Asterisk *
Used to set off a group of stitch instructions which are to be repeated across an entire row of knitting. Edge stitches may precede or follow the asterisks; only those between asterisks should be repeated.

Decrease (dec)
This is the process of reducing the number of stitches, and can be done in two ways. One: Slip the next stitch to be worked from the left needle to the right (without working it), work the next stitch, then slip the unworked stitch over the right nee-dle so that it forms a loop around the worked stitch. Two: Knit or purl two stitches together. The former method is normally used on left sloping decreases and the latter on right sloping ones. For detailed instructions, see page 31.

Dropped stitches
While a beginner may drop a stitch accidentally – it can usually be worked back on to the needle with the aid of a crochet hook – sometimes this has to be done to achieve a particular effect. It involves releasing the next loop from the left needle and allowing it to run as far as it will go.

Edge/side
To avoid confusion, 'edge' should be used to refer to the left or right selvedge of the work: the place where rows of knitting begin or end; 'side' means the surface area of the piece of work: right/wrong side or inside/outside.

Gauge
In order to assess exactly how the yarn you are using will work up, it is advisable to make a test swatch of knitting about 4 × 4 ins (10 × 10 cm) with the needles you propose to use. Yarn qualities and personal working tension vary a great deal and a few minutes spent on checking that your work will have the right number of rows to the inch or centimeter will be time well spent. In order to achieve a tighter tension, a slightly smaller needle should be tried, a larger one for looser tension. This is extremely important as the slightest error in tension will have a disastrous effect on the size of your finished garment.

Increase or increasing (inc)
The addition of one or more stitches on the needle. For detailed instructions see page 28.

Knit/purl through back loop (tbl)
This expression is used when a stitch is worked through the back instead of the front. This has the effect of twisting the stitch.

Parentheses ( )
Used to set off a group of instructions which are to be repeated a given number of times: (yo, sl 1, k 1, psso) four times.

Pass the slipped stitch over (psso)
This method is used to decrease width from the sides. Slip one stitch from left needle to right without working it; knit the next stitch; insert left needle into slipped stitch and draw it over the stitch just knitted and allow it to slide off the needle. Two or three stitches can be passed over a knitting stitch, if required.

Knit up (or pick up)
This expression has two meanings: i) working up, through the rows, a dropped stitch with the aid of a crochet hook or, ii) picking up and knitting stitches, evenly, around a neck edge or the edges of a jacket in order to add a border.

Repeat (rep)
This is usually accompanied by an asterisk which refers back to an asterisk earlier in the pattern, with the instruction "rep from * 3 times" (or whatever number is required). Sometimes the group of stitches to be repeated will be enclosed in parentheses.

Row
This word is constantly used in knitting instructions and refers to each set of stitches worked from one needle to the other. The initial casting on and final binding off are not counted as rows.

Selvedges
The two side edges of any piece of knitting are referred to as the selvedges and consist of the first and last stitch of each row.

Slip a stitch (sl st)
Pass one stitch from left needle to right without working it.

Stitch(es) (st(s))
This word has two meanings in knitting: i) each time the yarn is worked into a loop on the left needle and transferred to the right, this is one stitch made; and ii) a pattern consisting of one or more rows repeated to create a regular effect is called a stitch, i.e. garter stitch (every row is worked in knitting) or stockinette stitch (one row knit, one row purl).

Yarn forward/yarn back (yfwd/ybk)
Used to create many interesting textural effects, often with slipped stitches (see woven stitch patterns, pp 87-90). Unlike yarn over (yo), it does not make new or elongated stitches or holes in the work; rather it makes a firmer, denser knitted fabric.

Yarn over (yo)
The yarn is passed around the right needle before working the next stitch, thus adding one stitch to the row and making a hole in the work, especially useful in lacy stitch patterns. There may be a decrease to balance the yo, maintaining the stitch count. Or yarn overs may be dropped from the needle on the next row, resulting in an elongated stitch while maintaining the stitch count. Multiple yarn overs elongate stitches more; they are indicated as follows: (yo) twice, (yo) 3 times.

Beginning:
knit and purl

CASTING ON, BASIC STITCHES AND SPECIAL STITCHES

The position of the hands and needles is very important because, when the needles are maneuvered correctly, the work will proceed smoothly, with a regular rhythm and without tiring you.

A beginner is strongly advised to practice on a small piece of knitting, repeatedly undoing it, casting on and working a few rows. Complete mastery of the needles will produce a firm, easy tension which is easily recognized when the stitches slip fairly easily along the needle, when pushed, and the fabric produced is flexible and even. Patience at this stage will certainly be rewarded later.

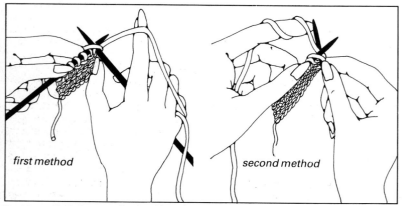

first method

second method

Position of knitting needles and hands

Position of the hands and needles

Before starting work, it is advisable to make sure that you are holding the knitting needles correctly. They should point forward with the knobbed ends projecting back towards the underarm on each side. There is a choice of working methods, however, and the first to be described is widely used throughout the world while the second is generally used in Central Europe. The main aim, of course, is to achieve the greatest possible speed with the least number of movements.

First method
1. The ball of wool is kept to the right and the right hand placed horizontally above the knitting needle. The yarn is passed round the little finger of this hand and over the other fingers. It should lie over the top joint of the index finger which controls the movement of the yarn.

2. The needle rests inside the hand on the curved middle and third fingers.

3. In working, it is the right thumb, helped by the little finger of the right hand, which guides the right needle towards the needle in the left hand.

4. The left hand remains fairly still, its main function being to hold the needle which carries all the stitches made in the previous row and to facilitate the making of each new stitch as it is slipped on to the right needle.

Second method (typical of Central Europe)

1. The ball of yarn is placed on the left. The yarn, carried over the little finger of the left hand, passes under the third and second fingers and then forms a ring round the index finger which must be kept close to the left needle to avoid unnecessary movements of the hand.

2. The right hand, placed horizontally over the right needle which it holds with the thumb and index finger, moves towards the yarn which is held taut by the first finger of the left hand in order that the stitch can be made.

Third method (the most commonly used but not illustrated)

1. The ball of yarn is kept on the right and the right needle rests between the thumb and index finger. The yarn is passed over the little finger, twisted round it, then brought under the two middle fingers and over the first finger. The yarn is kept over the first joint of the index finger, which plays a large part in guiding it over the right needle.

2. The right needle is pushed back and forth by the thumb and first finger as it rests lightly between them.

3. The second needle is held near the tip between the thumb and first finger of the left hand, the weight of the needle being taken by the other fingers which curve loosely round it.

4. The role of the left needle consists mainly of pushing the stitches to be worked forward, one by one, towards the needle held in the right hand. The latter, by means of a small movement of the first finger, makes the stitches.

Casting on

The process of forming the first series of loops on the left needle is called 'casting on'. The way this operation is carried out is vital to the success of any knitted item and it must therefore be done evenly and loosely to avoid pulling at the edges.

There are several methods of casting on. It must be stressed, however, that – whichever method of casting on is adopted – the stitches must be quite loose as they will form the edges of the pieces which will go to make up the garment. Elasticity is vital and it is often helpful to a beginner, who may tend to work too tightly at first, to use a much larger needle for casting on than will be used in the knitting itself. This loose casting on should not be exaggerated as the effect of an uneven edge is undesirable.

It is essential to select needles which are the right size and which are suited to the type of yarn being used. Test the tension and determine the type of fabric you wish to produce by making a swatch. (See 'Gauge', page 13).

Another important factor is the material from which knitting needles are made. If you tend to work rather tightly, keeping the yarn taut, metal needles enable the stitches to slide more easily than plastic; wooden needles may be preferable for openwork stitches in heavy yarns.

Different ways of casting on

Casting on may be done with one needle or with two. We will start by describing three ways of casting on with one needle only.

Thumb method – simple cast on

This method is generally used to increase the number of stitches at the sides of work rather than for basic casting on. Take one knitting needle into the right hand, keeping the ball of yarn on your left.

When practicing, leave a short length of yarn on the right side and

hold it firmly with the right hand – the work is done direct from the ball. No preliminary loop is necessary as the short length represents stitches of work which would normally already be on the needle. Carry the working yarn around the front of the left thumb, over the first finger and then let it lie over the palm of the hand where the third and fourth fingers will curl in to release the yarn and control the tension. You will now have a loop between your thumb and first finger. Now insert the needle under the back of the loop towards the center, to emerge behind the thumb. Release loop from left thumb and draw stitch up on needle. Repeat as required by replacing yarn on left thumb in the same position each time (this is easily done by a quick movement of the thumb in counter clockwise direction).

Normal method (also known as crossed casting)

This system is popular because it

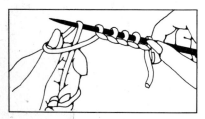

Thumb method – simple loop

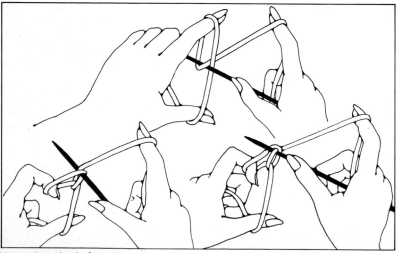

Normal method of casting on

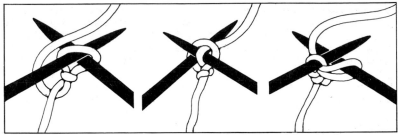

Casting on with two needles: first method, 'French method'

Casting on with two needles: second method, 'English method'

gives a firm yet elastic edge and is suitable for all kinds of yarn and all types of work. Special care must be taken in making the first stitch:

1. Keeping the ball of yarn to your right, pull out a length of yarn proportionate to the number of stitches you need.

2. Form a loop with the thumb and left forefinger.

3. Insert the knitting needle, held in the right hand, into the loop.

4. Still holding the loop extended with the left forefinger, with the right hand carry the yarn from the ball upwards over the needle.

5. Now bring the loop held by the left forefinger over the yarn just worked and then over and in front of the needle, finishing off the stitch by gently pulling the length of thread on the left.

Continue in the same way until the required number of stitches is on the needle.

Double casting on

This is a variation of the Normal method and is worked in the same way except that two strands are worked together from the left hand while only one remains on the needle for each stitch. It is especially suitable for heavier garments or anything that will receive especially hard wear.

When following this method, hold the two needles in the right hand and cast the stitches on to both of them. When all the stitches have been cast on, one of the needles is then withdrawn leaving the stitches fairly loose, although regular, to facilitate the working of the first row.

Two needle methods

Casting on with two needles is especially suitable when a large number of stitches is required and it would be difficult to calculate the length of yarn needed for the working strand. There are two methods which only vary in one respect from each other.

First method. This is sometimes called the 'French method' and is generally used when starting hems.

1. The first stitch is made as for the 'Normal method' (i.e. a slip-knot loop) but there is no need to leave a long tail on the left as all the stitches are made direct from the ball of yarn which is kept on your right side.

2. Transfer the first stitch from the right to the left needle which is held with the knob pointing towards the left armpit.

3. Insert the right needle through the front of the loop on the left needle, pass the yarn from back to front over the right needle and draw it back through the loop. Do not displace the first stitch from the left needle.

4. Now slip the loop just made on to the left needle; you now have two stitches. Pull up the yarn held in the right hand so that the stitch lies at a comfortable tension on the needle.

Insert the right needle into the second stitch, as above, and make another stitch, continuing thus until you have the required number of stitches on the left needle.

Second method. This is known as the 'English method' and is generally used for knitting in the round.

1. Work first two stitches as for the 'French method'.

2. Insert the right needle between the two stitches on the left needle.

3. Pass the yarn from back to front over the right needle and draw it back between the two stitches.

4. Now slip the stitch just made onto the left needle, on which there will now be three stitches. Pull up the yarn held in the right hand so that the stitch lies at a comfortably loose tension on the needle.

Insert the right needle between the last two stitches on the left needle, as above, and make another stitch in the same way, continuing thus until you have the required number of stitches on the left needle.

Casting on with four needles

Items such as socks, gloves and turtle necks are usually knitted on four double-pointed needles, which means that there is no seam as the knitting is worked 'in the round'. The stitches are divided as equally as possible between the needles.

1. The number of stitches cast on will depend upon the type of ribbing to be worked, i.e. an even number of stitches for single rib, multiples of 4 for double rib, multiples of 6 for triple rib, etc.

2. Cast the necessary number of stitches on to the first needle by whichever of the two needle systems you prefer. Now cast on an extra stitch, then transfer it onto another needle.

3. When the required number of stitches has been cast on to the latter needle, make an extra stitch and, as before, slip it on to the next needle.

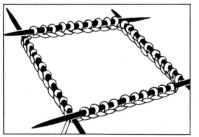

Method of casting on with four needles

4. With the third needle, cast on the balance of the stitches until all the stitches required are evenly distributed between the needles.

5. Holding the needles in such a way that they form a triangle (or a square, if five needles are being used), slip the first stitch from the first needle on to the last needle, thus closing the foundation for circular knitting.

Tubular stitch

This gives a very professional finish to the edges of cuffs, sweaters, wooly hats, etc., as the stitches are virtually invisible. It also involves a special method of knitting and of finishing off.

Casting on and knitting with the tubular stitch system

This method of casting on should only be attempted by a fairly experienced knitter as it calls for great precision. It is not really difficult, though, and can soon be mastered with a little patience and practice. There are two methods of casting on for the tubular system.

First method. This is the more usual method. Only one knitting needle is required and this is held in the right hand in the usual way, with the knobbed end pointing towards the armpit (or, if long enough, tucked under the arm). The ball of yarn is kept on your left side while a length of yarn – roughly proportionate to the number of stitches to be cast on – is controlled by the right hand.

1. Make the first stitch in the usual way. (This stitch will not be worked.)

2. With the left hand, carry the yarn from the ball upwards, from left to right, over the needle and down

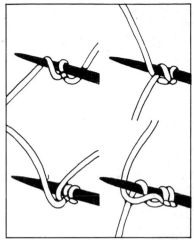

Casting on with the tubular stitch: first method

behind it.

3. Now, with the right hand, bring the loose yarn forward, in front of the other strand, carrying it from right to left under the point of the needle. (The first knit stitch has now been worked.)

4. With the left hand, carry the yarn from the ball over the needle again, in the same direction as in Step 2.

5. Now, with the right hand, bring the loose yarn back, behind the other strand, carrying it from left to right under the point of the needle. (The first purl stitch has now been worked.)

Repeat Steps 2-5 as required. The basic principle of this method of casting on is that the left hand carries the yarn around the needle while the right hand brings the loose yarn back and forth alternately towards the left and right, thus securing each stitch and forming a running thread at the same time.

The row should end with a purl stitch to enable the first row to be started with a knit stitch.

Before going on to describe the

alternative method of tubular stitch casting on, here is a brief explanation of how to continue working to complete the edging on the first tubular stitch method.

* Working only the knit stitches, slip each purl stitch as if to purl (that is, yarn forward, slip stitch from left to right needle, yarn back), continuing thus to the end of the row. *
Turn and repeat from * to * for two or three rows, when all the stitches will have been well secured. You will notice that the loop which was originally put on the needle to start casting on is now projecting slightly from one corner of the work. By gently pulling this loop, you will find that one of its two strands is a running thread and this should be carefully withdrawn, making the casting on stitches invisible. Continue working in single rib (see page 69), knitting one stitch into each knit stitch and one purl into each missed purl.

Second method. Two pairs of needles are required for this method of tubular stitch edging. One pair should be the size suitable for working the ribbing with the yarn being used while the second pair should be two sizes smaller and will be used only for the tubular edging. You will also need a small quantity of yarn in any contrasting color (this will be withdrawn later and can be re-used).

1. With contrasting yarn and the larger needles, cast on – by the normal method – half the actual number of stitches required.

2. Work in single rib (see page 69) for at least six rows, break off yarn and leave loose but do not tie it off.

3. Now, taking one of the smaller needles and the main yarn, but leaving a yarn tail long enough to finish off the edge, work (k1, p1) into each stitch to end of row. This will be the right side of the work and you

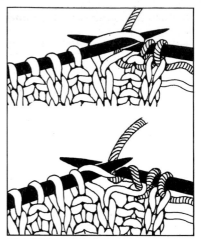

Casting on with the tubular stitch: second method

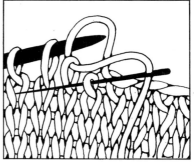

Binding off a tubular stitch edging

will have doubled the number of stitches.

4. With the larger needles, continue in tubular stitch (see First Method) for at least four rows and then in single rib until the required depth of ribbing has been worked.

5. Holding the contrasting colored thread between thumb and forefinger, pull it firmly and cut it off close to the work. Now detach the part knitted in the contrasting color.

Binding off a tubular stitch edging

With a yarn needle and the main color yarn still attached to the work, each stitch is worked separately off the knitting needle as follows:

1. The first stitch is a knit stitch so insert the yarn needle into it as if to purl and slip it off the knitting needle.
2. The second stitch will also be a knit stitch but this should be taken as if to knit and slipped off.
3. Now insert the yarn needle into the first stitch of the row again – i.e. the first stitch to have been slipped on to your working yarn – then purlwise into the third stitch (the next on the knitting needle, which will be a knit stitch) and slip it off the knitting needle.
4. Insert the yarn needle into the second stitch of the row i.e. the second stitch to have been slipped on to your working thread – and then knitwise into the fourth stitch (the next on the knitting needle, which will be a purl stitch) and slip it off the knitting needle.

These four steps are repeated to the end of the row.

Basic stitches

The following are used to make up all the more complex stitches but they are, in themselves, the simplest and most widely used. Whole garments are frequently designed entirely in these basic stitches and can be very effective, especially when yarns are used which have particularly interesting textures or color blends.

To knit

Hold the needle containing the cast-on stitches in the left hand and the second needle in the right hand. The yarn should be held in the right hand, and kept to the back of the work.

Insert the right needle from left to right through the front of the first stitch on the left needle, pass the yarn around the point of the right needle, draw it through and slip the first stitch off the left needle.

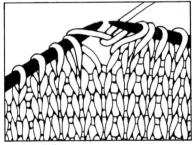

Knitting

To purl

This stitch produces a ridge on the front of the work which looks exactly the same as the back of a knit row. It is therefore seldom used by itself but in conjunction with knit stitches, either in alternate rows or in the same row. This will become clearer as you start to read the explanations of stitches further on in the book.

Hold the needle containing the

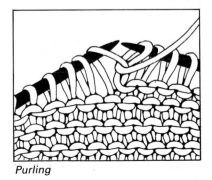

Purling

cast-on stitches in the left hand and the second needle in the right hand. The yarn should be held in the right hand, as already described, and kept to the front of the work.

* Insert the right needle from right to left through the front of the first stitch on the left needle, pass yarn around the point of the right needle, draw it through (thus making a loop on the right needle) and slip the first loop off the left needle. Repeat from * until all the stitches have been worked off the left on to the right needle.

At the end of the row, turn the work and continue in whatever stitch is required.

When purling, the yarn should be kept to the front of the work.

Twisted knitting

This is worked in the same way as ordinary knitting except that the right needle is inserted from right to left into the back of the stitch.

Twisted purling

This is worked in the same way as ordinary purling except that the right needle is inserted upwards into the back of the stitch.

Garter stitch

Garter stitch is the simplest of all to work and is as effective when using the thicker yarns for heavy knits and casual clothes as it is for the soft, finer yarns such as mohair which require a delicate, elegant look.

Garter stitch is worked entirely in the knit stitch. If a particularly firm fabric is required, this can be achieved by knitting into the back of each stitch.

Twisted knitting

Twisted purling

Garter stitch

Stockinette stitch

Both sides look identical with this stitch.

Stockinette stitch (st st)

This is the most classical stitch in knitting and the most frequently used, as it lends itself to all styles of garment and all types of yarn.

Stockinette stitch consists of alternate rows of knit and purl, which gives a smooth effect on one side (the knit side) and a ridged effect on the other (the purl side). Either side may be used as the right side, depending upon the general effect required. Using the purl side as the right side is known as reversed stockinette stitch (r st st).

Special stitches

Under this heading is a number of variations which are neither knit nor purl. They will be found frequently in the stitch combinations of the various patterns that follow in the book and are an essential part of any knitting, whether following a standard design or making up your own.

Yarn over (yo)

A yarn over produces an extra stitch but is not an ordinary increase, as it is usually compensated for by a decrease. There are various ways in which yarn overs can be made and great care must always be taken to execute them correctly.

Yarn over after a knit stitch

To work a yarn over between two knit stitches, knit the first stitch, bring the yarn forward under the point of the right-hand needle, then back over the top of the needle and knit the second stitch.

For a yarn over between a knit and a purl stitch, knit the first stitch, bring the yarn forward under the point of the right needle, over the top of the needle and forward again under the point. The yarn will have made a complete loop around the needle.

Yarn over after a purl stitch

If a yarn over has to be worked between a purl and a knit stitch, when the purl stitch has been worked, take the yarn back over the right needle and knit the next stitch as usual.

If a yarn over has to be worked between two purl stitches, when the first one has been worked take the yarn back over the right needle and forward again under the point. The yarn will now have made a complete loop around the needle and will be in the correct position for purling the next stitch.

Multiple yarn overs

Double, triple and more yarn overs are made by carrying the yarn around the needle the required number of times, in the same direction as for a single yarn over. See 'Elongating a stitch' (page 27).

Crossing the stitches (cable stitch)

This consists of knitting stitches in the opposite order to that in which they appear on the needle. The explanation here is for single stitches only but when several are to be crossed, a short double-pointed needle is used to carry the stitches forward or back (a cable needle). Stitches may be crossed on a knit or a purl row and to the left or the right.

Crossing stitches to the left on a knit row

*Insert the right needle into the front of the second stitch on the left needle, passing behind the first stitch; knit it without removing it from the needle. Now knit the first stitch and allow both to slip off left needle.

Crossing stitches to the right on a plain row

Insert the right needle into front of the second stitch on left needle, passing in front of the first stitch; knit it without removing it from the needle. Knit the first stitch and allow both stitches to slip off left needle.

Crossing stitches to the left on a purl row

Slip the first stitch on to a cable needle and hold it in front of the work. Purl the next stitch, replace the slipped stitch on to the left needle and purl it.

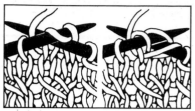

Crossed stitches to the left on a knit row

Crossed stitches to the right on a knit row

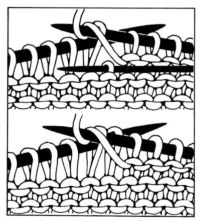

Crossed stitches to the left (above) and to the right (below) on a purl row

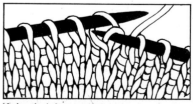

Knit stitch in row below

Crossing stitches to the right on a purl row

Insert the right needle into front of the second stitch on left-hand needle, passing in front of the first stitch, and purl it without removing it from the needle. Now purl the first stitch and allow both stitches to slip off the left needle.

Knit stitch in row below

This type of work is often found in the composition of stitches. It can be found, for example, in the English rib (see page 66) and the Honeycomb stitch (see page 78). Working in knitting, insert the right needle into the center of the stitch below the stitch being worked – that is, the stitch of the previous row – and knit both together.

Slipped stitches – knitwise and purlwise (or slip as if to knit or to purl)

To slip a stitch knitwise, insert the right needle into the next stitch on the left needle as though you were going to knit it but do not pass the yarn around it. Simply transfer the stitch on to the right needle.

To slip a stitch purlwise, insert the needle as though about to purl the next stitch and transfer it to the right needle.

Passing the slipped stitch over (psso)

This operation is used to decrease the number of stitches and may be worked in knit or purl.

Slip one stitch (as if to knit or as if to purl, according to the design).

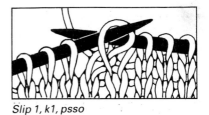

Slip 1, k1, psso

Elongated stitch

Work the next stitch, then lift the slipped stitch over it with the aid of the left needle.

Double decrease: Knitting (or purling) two stitches together and psso (sl1, k2 tog, psso)

This operation decreases the number of stitches by two.

Slip one stitch (knitwise or purlwise), knit (or purl) the next two stitches together, lift the slipped stitch over stitch just completed, with the aid of the left needle.

Elongating a stitch

This method is used to give an openwork effect.

Insert the right needle into the next stitch, carry the yarn around the right needle two or three times, finish the stitch in the normal way. On the return row, drop all the extra loops as each stitch is worked, thus elongating it.

INCREASING DECREASING AND FINISHING

Increasing and decreasing

It is essential to master the techniques of increasing and decreasing in order to make any knitted articles that are not either square or rectangular, such as scarves or afghans.

The number of stitches can be increased on the outside edges (shaping) or within the individual pieces that go to make up a garment (fashioning).

The number of stitches can also be decreased on the outside edges or from the inside.

Increasing on outside edge

To increase at the beginning or end of a row, use the simple thumb method to cast on the required number of extra stitches.

Increasing from the inside

Single or double increasing is worked in the course of a row and may be done in different ways, sometimes even creating decorative effects.

Single internal increase

Knit a stitch in the usual way but, before slipping the loop from the left needle, bring the yarn forward and work one purl stitch into the same stitch. This completes one increase.

A single internal increase can be worked symmetrically at both edges of a piece of work. To do this, work the increase on the third stitch from the start of the row and on the third stitch from the end.

Single internal pick-up increase

A pick-up increase is worked by knitting the stitch from the previous row as well as the stitch on the needle.

To get a symmetrical increase on both sides of the work, pick up the extra stitch before knitting the third stitch from the start of the row and after knitting the third loop from the end.

Single internal between-stitch increase

This increase is made by picking up with the right needle the horizontal thread linking two stitches, transferring it to the left needle and working a twisted knit stitch into it (i.e. knitting into the back of it). If the extra stitch is knitted normally (i.e. from the front), a small hole is formed which is sometimes used to create a decorative openwork effect.

To increase symmetrically at the sides by this method, knit up the

Single internal increase

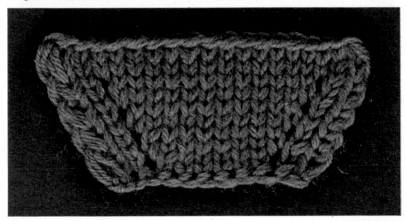

Single internal pick-up increase

Single internal between-stitch increase

Single internal openwork increase

Double openwork increase

linking thread between the third and fourth stitches from the start of the row and between the fourth and third stitches from the end of the row.

Single internal increase with openwork

This is worked by putting the yarn over the needle, making a yarn over (yo) which is purled on the return row, forming an openwork design.

To obtain symmetrical increases, a yo is made after working the third stitch from the start of the row and another before working the third stitch from the end of the row.

Double increases

These are worked in the same way as the single increases except that they are worked in pairs, one on each side of the central stitch which forms a center line for the increases. Double increases are used when working pleats and anything which necessitates perfect symmetry.

Decreasing on outside edges

Slip the first stitch, knit (or purl) the second and pass the slipped stitch over it. To decrease two stitches, after slipping the first stitch work the next two together and pass the slipped stitch over.

To obtain a neater edge, slip the last stitch of the row on to the right needle without working it, turn, work the slipped stitch, slip the second, pass the first stitch over it.

Decreasing from the inside

This operation is carried out as a row is being worked and the decreases may be single or double.

Single internal decreases sloping left or right on right side of work

Decreases towards the left are worked by slipping a stitch knitwise, knitting the next stitch and passing the slipped stitch over. The same type of decrease is achieved by knitting into the backs of two loops together, although this gives a slightly raised effect.

Decreases sloping towards the right are made by knitting two stitches together in the normal way, that is, by inserting the right needle into the second loop and then into the first loop on the left needle and then by working a plain stitch.

Single internal decreases sloping left or right on wrong side of work

In this case, although the decreases are made from the back of the work,

Single internal decreases sloping left or right on front of work

Double internal decreases sloping left or right on front of work

the sloping line will appear on the front. For a decrease to the left, slip the last stitch worked from the right needle to the left needle. slip the second loop over it (from left to right) and return stitch to right needle.

For a decrease to the right, purl two stitches together.

Double decreases

A double decrease reduces the number of stitches by two in one operation. It is used to obtain a neat point at the angle of a V-neck and in some decorative stitches.

Double internal decrease sloping left or right on right side of work

A left slant is obtained by knitting

into the backs of three stitches together to make one stitch. (All three loops will slip off the needle at the same time.)

A right slant is obtained by knitting three stitches together in the normal way, i.e. insert the right needle as if to knit into the third, second and first stitches on the left needle, to make one stitch. (All three loops will slip off the needle at the same time.)

Double internal decreases, sloping left or right, using psso's

To decrease two stitches and make a left-sloping stitch, slip one stitch, knit next two together and psso.

To decrease two stitches and make a right-sloping stitch, slip one stitch as if to knit, knit the second stitch and pass the slipped stitch over it; now transfer the stitch just made from the right needle to the left and pass the next stitch over it from left to right; replace the previously made stitch onto right needle.

Double vertical internal decreases, using psso's

Insert right needle as if to knit into second and first loops (in that order) on left needle and slip them both on to right needle; knit the next stitch and pass slipped stitches over it.

Double internal decreases sloping left or right on wrong side of work

Although the decreases are worked on the wrong side, the sloping stitches will appear on the right side.

To work a left-sloping double de-

crease, purl two stitches together and transfer the stitch just made to the left needle; pass the next loop over it from left to right and replace the previously made stitch on to right needle.

To work a right-sloping double decrease, purl three stitches together; as this has been worked on the wrong side, the sloping stitch will appear on the right side of the work.

Double internal decreases sloping left or right on wrong side of work

Selvedges and borders

Selvedges are formed from the first and last stitch of each row and it is important for them to be worked evenly in order to ensure the success of the finished article.

Borders are also extremely important. They may either be worked in with the main knitting, or worked separately and sewn on, or worked on picked-up stitches.

Chain selvedge

Slipped or chain selvedge

When working on the right side, slip the first stitch of each row as if to knit and knit the last stitch; when working on the wrong side, slip the first stitch of each row as if to purl and purl the last stitch.

Slipped garter stitch selvedge

Slip the first stitch of every row as if to knit and knit the last stitch of every row, including wrong side rows.

Selvedge to be flat-seamed

Knit the first and last stitch of every right side row and purl the first and last stitch of every wrong side row.

Beaded selvedge

Beaded or slipped double garter stitch selvedge

Slip the first stitch as if to knit through back loop; keeping yarn at back of work, knit the next stitch. Knit the last two stitches of row. This is repeated throughout, including on wrong side rows.

Picked-up stitches

Edgings on collars, pockets, etc., are often worked by picking up stitches from the edges and working on these to create a finished border worked directly on to the fabric, in the same or a contrasting color.

The stitches may be picked up directly with a knitting needle (a finer one than is to be used for the knitting is recommended); or with the aid of a crochet hook used in the following way: insert the hook into the stitch to be picked up, take yarn round hook draw it through the stitch and transfer the newly-made stitch to a knitting needle. Continue in this way until the required number of stitches has been picked up evenly.

Picking up stitches

Incorporated garter stitch border

This may be started at the beginning of the work – on the lower edge of the pieces that will make up a jacket, wrist edges of sleeves, etc. In the case of the two fronts for a jacket, six or so stitches can be worked in garter stitch along the center of both fronts. The last stitch of the border should always be purled on the wrong side, to give a stockinette stitch effect along the edge.

Picked-up garter stitch border

Incorporated seed stitch border

The instructions for incorporated garter stitch border may be followed except that seed stitch (page 76) replaces garter stitch.

Incorporated single rib border

The instructions for incorporated garter stitch border may be followed except that single (k1 p1) rib replaces garter stitch, and first stitch should be slipped (not worked).

Picked-up single rib border

Garter stitch border on picked-up stitches

Pick up the number of stitches required and work in garter stitch until the border reaches the necessary width, ending with a row on the

wrong side. Now, with the right side facing you, knit the first stitch, *transfer it to left needle, knit 2 sts together and transfer the stitch onto left needle *. Repeat from * to * to end of row.

Single rib border on picked-up stitches

Work in k1 p1 rib, on the picked-up

stitches until the required border width is reached. For this style of border, it is advisable to use the tubular method for the last four rows and binding off (see page 22).

Crocheted borders

Crocheted borders are often used to finish a knitted article. They are worked directly onto the fabric and always add an elegant touch of professionalism to the garment. The two examples given here are used later in the book.

Corded (or reverse single crochet) edge

Corded (or reverse single crochet stitch) edge

Work one row in single crochet (insert hook into stitch, yarn over hook, draw loop through, yarn over hook and draw through both loops on hook). Do not turn.

Work a second row in reverse single crochet stitch which means single crochet from left to right.

Picot edge

Work a row in single crochet (see previous instructions), then one more row as follows: * 3 single crochet, 3 chain (made by passing the hook under the yarn and pulling a loop out through the loop on the hook), 1 single crochet into the first of the 3 chain *. Repeat from * to * to end of the row.

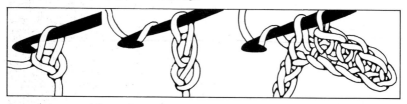

Crocheted chain and single crochet

Picot edge

Hems and corners

Hems can be worked in any decorative stitch but the part to be folded under should always be in stockinette stitch in order not to make the hem too bulky.

Corners or points can give a nicely finished off appearance to almost any garment. They may be worked as an integral part of the knitting, by picking up stitches (that is to say, worked from the inner edge outwards), or they may be worked separately and attached when the main fabric of a garment has been completed (that is to say, worked from the outer edge inwards).

Simple hem

Cat's tooth hem

Simple hem

Cast on by the simple thumb method, keeping the work quite loose, and work in stockinette stitch to the depth required for the hem. Now work a purl row on the right side of work (this will form a ridge and indicate where the fold will be). Continue in main pattern until the work reaches the same depth as the first part of the hem; fold the work in half with the wrong side inside and knit one row in pattern but picking up one stitch from the cast-on edge with each stitch knitted.

Cat's tooth hem

Cast on an odd number of stitches and work in stockinette stitch for the depth required for the hem.

Now work a row of holes as follows: k1, * yarn over (yo), k2 tog *. Repeat from * to * to end of row.

Continue working in pattern and, when the work is finished, turn up the hem at the openwork row and sew neatly into place.

Right-angle corners

These are simple to work when knitted at the same time as the main fabric. Use a stitch to contrast with the main pattern and ensure that the width of the side border is the same as the depth of the lower border – this means that the number of stitches worked as a side border has to be calculated to measure the same as the number of rows in lower border.

Corners worked from the outer edge inwards

These are worked on five stitches, the third of which forms the center of the corner. On right side of work, k2 tog, k1 (center stitch), k2 tog. Turn. On wrong side of work, k1, p1, k1. Continue in this way on each corner for depth of border.

For a more acute angle, decreases must also be made on the wrong side of the work.

For a wider-angled corner, it is only necessary to decrease on every fourth row.

Openwork corners worked from the outer edge inwards

These are worked on five stitches, the third of which forms the center of the corner. On right side of work, k2 tog, yo, k1 (central st), yo, k2 tog. On wrong side of work, k2 tog, p1 (central st), k2 tog. Continue in this way on each corner for depth of border.

For a more acute angle, work on seven stitches and k3 tog on right side. Work wrong side as above.

For a wider angled corner, work on five stitches but decrease on wrong side only every fourth row. Work right side as in first paragraph above.

Right-angle corner

Corner worked from outside in

Corner worked from outside in with openwork design

Corner worked from the inside edge outwards

This type of corner is worked by picking up the stitches on the edges of the knitted fabric already made and increasing at each side of the stitch that will be the center of the corner. This stitch should be marked with a contrasting yarn so that it is easily distinguishable.

On right side of work, work inc 1 to right of center (marked) stitch, knit center st, inc 1 to left of center st.

On wrong side of work, purl all 3 corner sts.

Continue in this way on each corner for depth of border.

For a more acute angle, it is only necessary to increase on every fourth row.

For a wider angled corner, work increases on every row (on wrong side as well as right side).

Buttonholes and pockets

Buttonholes are very much in evidence and must be worked neatly. They should always be finished off in buttonhole stitch, using the main yarn, and may be vertical or horizontal.

Pockets are also very important finishing touches to a garment and may often be a main feature. They, too, must be worked carefully, whether made as patch-pockets or incorporated into the main fabric either vertically or horizontally.

Vertical buttonholes

At the point where a buttonhole is required, the work is divided in two, one part left on a spare needle while the rest is continued until the required depth is reached. These stitches are left while the first part is knitted for the same number of rows.

Horizontal buttonholes

At the point where a buttonhole is required, bind off a few stitches on right side of work, to the width of the buttons. On return row work as far as bound off stitches; turn work and cast on the same number of stitches as were bound off; turn work again and complete row.

Vertical buttonhole

Horizontal buttonhole

Buttonholes for baby clothes

On a right side row at the exact point where a buttonhole is required yo, k2 tog. On return row work both stitches back into pattern.

Patch-pockets

When the garment is finished, knit pocket(s) to size required and sew on with very small stitches in the same yarn as the pocket.

Incorporated horizontal pockets

Where the pocket is to be started, in the same stitch as the cuffs, collar, etc, work a few rows for the pocket border and bind off fairly loosely. Work the pocket lining by casting on as many stitches as the pocket border plus four; work in stockinette stitch for the depth required, binding off two stitches at the beginning of the last two rows. Return to main knitting and knit in the stitches of the pocket lining. Stitch in place.

Patch-pocket

Incorporated horizontal pocket

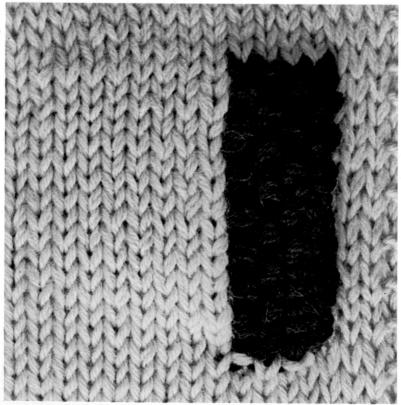

Incorporated vertical pocket

Incorporated vertical pockets

Divide the work (leaving one part on a spare needle) at the point where the side opening of the pocket will be. Continue working on the part of knitting where the pocket is to be made; the first six stitches should be in the same stitch as the cuffs, collar, etc. When the required depth has been reached, put aside. Cast on stitches for pocket lining to match the desired width of pocket and work in stockinette stitch to required size. Complete the work left on spare needle to the same depth as the pocket. Now transfer pocket lining stitches to a double-pointed needle and, placing them parallel with the top of the pocket work them together with the corresponding stitches on the top of the pocket.

Tailored (or 'afterthought') pocket (horizontal)

Run a contrasting piece of yarn through the stitches on both sides of a center line where the pocket is required. Cut and draw a thread out along the line to the necessary width and pick up the stitches on the lower edge of the opening. Work a border in the same stitch as cuffs, collar, etc. Make a pocket lining and graft (see page 58) the stitches to those of the upper edge of the opening.

Necklines, collars and sleeves

The following explanations cover only the classical necklines and collars but you will find several variations described individually in the main text.

Sleeves are usually started from the cuff, which should always be well-fitting but flexible; working towards the underarm, an extra stitch (inc 1) must be made every 1–1½ ins. (3–4 cm) at each side of the knitting. When the required length is reached, the shaping for the armhole begins.

Round neckline

This is the classic neckline which is suitable for any design and, once the basic stitches have been picked up, almost any style of collar can be worked into it. Allow a depth of approximately 2–2½ ins (6–7 cm) below shoulders for a round neck.

For the front, when the required length has been reached above armhole shaping either bind off or leave on a stitch holder about the center one-third of the stitches on the needle. The two side pieces are worked separately. Continue working on one neck edge, decreasing one stitch every second row until the required number of stitches for shoulder has been reached. Work remaining neck edge to correspond.

Picked-up band on round neckline

When the neckline has been worked on front and back, join the two pieces together. With a set of double-pointed needles (see page 20) pick up and knit all the stitches from around the neck edge; work in the same stitch as for the cuffs until required depth is reached. Cast off loosely as this edge needs to be very

Round neck with picked-up ribbed edging and set-in sleeve

stretchy to pass comfortably over the head.

V-neck

Divide the knitting in half by binding off the center stitch and leaving one half of the stitches on a spare needle. Now work on the other half, decreasing one stitch every four rows at neck edge by working the 3rd and 4th sts together. The two neck edge stitches should be worked in stockinette stitch. Work the other side to match.

Border for V-neck

When the neckline has been made and the back is finished, with a set of double-pointed needles pick up all the stitches evenly around neckline. Work to required depth, working double vertical decreases at center point (see page 33).

Square neck

When the depth at which the neckline is to begin is reached, bind off all the center front stitches to the width required. Continue straight in main pattern, on each side separately, as far as the top of the shoulders.

Picked-up band on square neckline

When neckline is completed, join front and back pieces and, with a set of double-pointed needles (see page 20), pick up evenly and knit all the stitches around neck edge. Work in rounds in the same rib as cuffs for the required depth, working double internal decreases (see page 32) at corners.

Mock turtle or turtle neck

Working on a round neck pick up evenly all the stitches on a set of

44

double-pointed needles and work in rib for 6½–7 ins (15–16 cm) for a turtle neck or about 3½–4 ins (8–9 cm) for a mock turtle neck.

Classic round armhole

Back and front: on the right side of work decrease 3 sts at each side, work return row (wrong side); * dec 2 sts at each side, work return row *, rep from * to * once; dec 1 st at each side. Continue without shaping to top of shoulders.

Sleeve: on the right side of fabric decrease 3 sts at each side, work return row (wrong side); * dec 2 sts at each side, work return row *, rep from * to * once; dec 1 st at each side, work return row. Now decrease 1 st at the beginning of every row until a quarter of the original number of stitches remain. Bind off.

The depth of the armhole at front and back must be the same.

Raglan sleeve

Back and front: make a note of the number of stitches. On the right side of fabric, decrease 3 sts at each side, work return row (wrong side); dec 2 sts at each side, work return row. Continue decreasing 1 st at both ends of every right side row until the neck is reached.

Divide the original number of stitches by three and bind off the central third. Continue working one side, decreasing one stitch at armhole

V-neck with picked-up ribbed border

Turtle neck collar picked up and worked on 4 needles

Openwork pattern worked into raglan sleeve

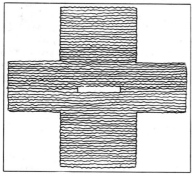

Garment with kimono sleeves

edge of every right side row until 1 st remains. Fasten off. Return to other side and complete to match.

Sleeve: on the right side of fabric, dec 3 sts at each side, work return row (wrong side); dec 2 sts at each side, work return row. Continue decreasing 1 st at both ends of every right side row until 8–10 stitches

remain. Bind off.

The armhole depth on the back and front pieces and on the sleeve must be the same.

Dropped shoulder line

The back and front pieces of a garment are made perfectly straight to the top of the shoulders, with no armhole shapings.

The sleeves are bound off when they are the required length.

Kimono sleeves

Kimono sleeves are worked in one piece with the front and back pieces of the garment. The knitting may be worked horizontally (starting from the lower edge of the front or back) or vertically (starting from the cuffs).

Horizontally: From the armpits, on

Sleeve built into yoke

right side of work, inc 2 sts at both ends of row, work return row; inc 3 sts at both ends, work return row. Now cast on, with the simple thumb method, the number of stitches for the length of sleeve required.

Work until neck opening is reached. Bind off as many stitches as required from the center of the row. Work a few rows (an even number) on left-hand stitches and break off yarn. Return to right-hand stitches and work the same number of rows. Turn work, cast on the same number of stitches bound off for neck opening, and continue to end of row.

Continue working until second half of sleeves is as deep as first half and bind off the same number of stitches from each side as were previously cast on. Then decrease 3 sts once at both ends of a right side row, work return row; dec 2 sts once

at both ends; continue working until fabric measures the same as the first straight piece worked. Bind off.

Vertically: Knitting starts from the wrist edge of a sleeve and, when the armpit is reached, the stitches are cast on for the back and front sections.

Yoke sleeve

This is particularly suitable for baby clothes. The front, back and sleeves are worked as far as the armpits, each piece being slipped on to a spare needle or stitch holder when finished. Arrange all the stitches (with garment pieces in this order: front, sleeve, back, sleeve) onto a set of double-pointed needles and work, in the round, decreasing 1 st where the sleeves join the front and back until the required depth of work is reached. Bind off loosely.

Pleats and 'darts'

The only difficulty about making knitted pleats is in calculating how many stitches to cast on and it is therefore helpful to be able to check with a previously made example. If this is not possible, then it is well worth spending a little time making a few small test pieces until it is possible to estimate how many stitches will be needed for the size required.

Darts are always made by decreasing or increasing, never stitched, in knitting. They may be vertical or horizontal. Careful calculations must be made on sizing as it is not possible to put hems on knitted pleats.

Inverted pleats lying to the left

The stitches are worked in groups to produce the width and depth of the pleats which are defined by two stitches worked on every right side row, one of which is slipped as if to knit and the other purled to form the edges of the pleat and the line at the back.

One pleat, with a width, front and back, of five stitches, is worked on 18 sts as follows:

1st row: * sl 1 as if to knit, k5, p1, k11 *.

Inverted pleats lying to the right and left

2nd row: * p11, k1, p6 *.

Rep these two rows until required length is reached. The pleats are now bound off as follows: * With right side of work facing you, transfer the slipped stitch and 5 knitted stitches onto a spare needle; onto another spare needle, transfer the purl stitch and the next 5 knitted stitches. Now, with all three needles held parallel, and the 1st needle nearest to you (right side of work), knit one stitch off each needle all together. Repeat from * to * for each pleat.

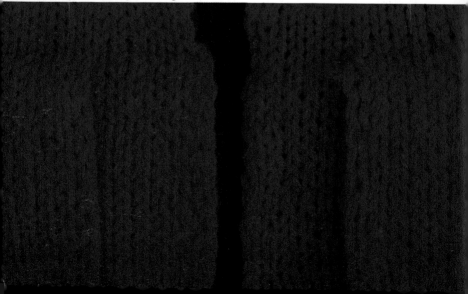

False or 'sun-ray' pleats and box pleats

Inverted pleats lying to the right

These are worked in the same way but reversing the stitch grouping:
1st row: * p1, k5, sl1 as if to knit, k11*.
2nd row: * p17, k1*.

Box pleats

These are worked in the same way as normal pleats (see previous two instructions) except that one fold is worked to the left and one to the right on each pleat. This is achieved by doubling the number of stitches in pleat width and adding 2 extra stitches for depth of folds. One box pleat of 5 stitches, front and back, is worked on 36 stitches as follows:
1st row: * k5, sl1 as if to knit, k5, p1, k12, p1, k5, sl1 as if to knit, k5 *.
2nd row: * p11 k1, p12, k1, p11 *.

Imitation or 'sun-ray' pleats

Starting from lower edge of skirt – usually working on a circular needle, to avoid seams – work in rib * k8 (9 or 10), p3 *. Every 8–10 rows (on right side of work) k2 tog just before working the p3. Continue in this way until required length and waist measurement are reached.

Single vertical 'darts'

When darts are required to narrow the garment, work as follows: mark the stitch which will form the line of the dart; on next and every fourth row, work 2 sts together just before the marked stitch.

To widen the garment, the same principle applies except that increases are worked instead of decreases.

Double vertical 'darts'

For darts that will narrow the garment, mark the stitch which will form the line of the dart, with contrasting yarn; on next and every 3rd row work 2 sts together just before the marked stitch (this will give alternating decreases on the right and wrong sides of the work, on each side of the central stitch).

For darts that will widen the garment, the same principle applies except that increases are worked instead of decreases.

Horizontal 'darts'

These are sometimes used on the outer edges to shape work such as shoulders or bust line.

The principle is to turn the work about 4 sts before the end of the row; sometimes the turn is made on alternate rows, at evenly spaced points starting about 4 sts from the end of the row, then 8, 12, etc. This gives a gently curved line to give shaping over the bust. The exact point at which turns are made depends, of course, upon the thickness of the yarn and amount of shaping required.

Binding off, repairing, trimming, blocking and finishing

Besides the usual finishing touches that are used to complete a knitted garment, there are various original ideas and techniques which can be adapted to give individuality to anything you make – decorative trimmings such as tassels, pompons and fringes are easy to make.

Especially useful is the 'know-how' on how to remedy mistakes in the knitting and to repair a new garment that has been damaged or a favorite old one that is wearing out.

As soon as all the pieces of a garment have been completed, in most cases the first thing to do is to block them. Then comes sewing together. Both these operations are important and the greatest care must be taken with them. The results will make it all worthwhile.

Binding off

Binding off is the operation carried out on the last row of the various pieces that go to make up almost any article. It merely means that each stitch is securely finished off. It is very important to keep the thread rather loose to ensure that all bound-off edges are elastic; tight edges can ruin any garment, however well it has been knitted otherwise.

There are several methods of binding off, some more complicated than others.

First method This is the most usual system and is sometimes cal-

led the French method. All the stitches must be bound off as they have been worked (i.e. knit stitches are bound off as if to knit, and purl as if to purl). K2, pass the first of these over the second and off needle (this leaves one new st on right needle); *work another stitch and pass the stitch already on needle over it *. Repeat from * to * until 1 st remains. Fasten off by breaking thread and passing it through loop, slip loop off needle and draw thread up firmly.

Second method This is a useful system for anyone who is a particularly tight knitter or if an especially elastic, flat edge is required (i.e. for patch-pockets, knitted-on borders, etc.) K2 stitches, * pass the first st over second st but leave the first st on the left needle; work the next stitch on left needle but do not slip the previous bound-off stitch off the left needle until the new stitch has been completed. Repeat from * to * until 1 stitch remains. Fasten off.

Third method This is sometimes called the English method. It gives a slightly raised effect and is firm without being tight. It is particularly suitable for edges that have to be seamed such as the yoke of a dress which will have to be sewn on with a flat seam.

Knit 2 tog through back of stitches. *Slip this stitch from right to left needle and knit it together with next stitch through the back of both stitches *. Repeat from * to * until 1 stitch remains. Fasten off.

Picking up a dropped stitch

If you should happen to drop a stitch as you are working it is not difficult to pick it up again, with a little care, thus avoiding the necessity of undoing the work.

Using a crochet hook of a suitable size for the thickness of yarn, catch the dropped stitch and work it up through the horizontal bars until you reach the row being worked, and slip it onto the needle in its correct position. A dropped knitted stitch will be in front of the horizontal bar and a purled one will be behind it.

How to divide a piece of knitting

It is sometimes necessary to cut a knitted garment right across, from one side to the other, in order to renew the lower part. In the case of a newly knitted article, this may be because one piece has ended up longer/shorter than another, when

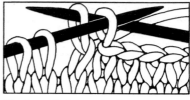
Binding off: 1st method

Binding off: 2nd method

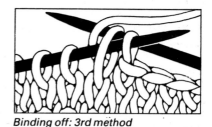
Binding off: 3rd method

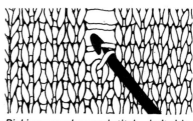
Picking up a dropped stitch – knit side

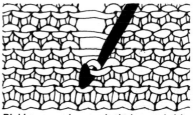
Picking up a dropped stitch – purl side

they should have been equal, or – in the case of an old favorite – part of it may have been torn or worn out. However, there is no need to do the work all over again. With right side of work towards you, just pull a thread on the right-hand edge where you wish to divide the work until the whole width of the knitting is firmly gathered; now break the thread on the left-hand edge and allow all the stitches to slip off. The knitting will have fallen into two parts. All you have to do now is to pick up all the stitches and continue working on them until the required length is reached. Bind off. (Works only on stockinette or garter stitch.)

A favorite knitted garment can easily be given a new lease of life by following this method and inserting a border in a contrasting color or an interesting stitch.

If the lower part does not have to be re-knitted, the detached piece can be joined again by grafting it with a length of the main yarn and a yarn needle (see page 58).

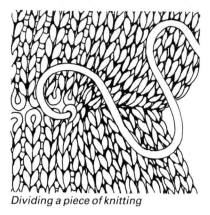

Dividing a piece of knitting

Repairing knitting

Any knitted garment that has been well worn may become a little threadbare in parts, especially the elbows of sweaters or jackets, or a hole may develop where a strand has been pulled or broken. It is not difficult to reinforce or mend the weak area or hole, if a small amount of yarn has been retained from the making. The repair is carried out in two stages: the first is preparatory and the second is the mend itself.

Here we deal with mending worked on the right side of stockinette stitch for which there are two methods.

For either method, the worn place must be prepared and old stitches removed where they are thin. Cut the worn threads, thus freeing the stitches, making sure they form an even edge on the vertical sides. The result should be a square or rectangular hole with horizontal bars. Free 2-4 stitches at each corner, turn them to back of work and stitch securely in place.

First method On wrong side of work and using a darning needle, lay a thread horizontally for each row of stitches to be replaced, carrying each thread slightly beyond the edge. When this preparatory work has been completed, bring the needle through to the right side of work, as near as possible to the sound part on the left. Working downwards, take up the nearest horizontal thread from below upwards, keeping the working thread to the left of the needle. Continue until all the threads of the foundation have been covered.

When the last thread has been worked over, pass the needle downwards to the left of the nearest stitch and bring it out to the right of the same stitch.

From this point, the stitches are worked upwards, still keeping the yarn to the left of the needle. When

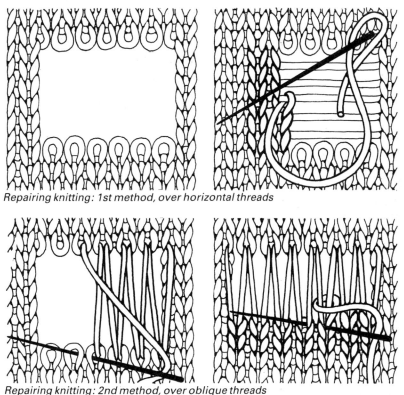

Repairing knitting: 1st method, over horizontal threads

Repairing knitting: 2nd method, over oblique threads

the last horizontal bar has been reached, insert the needle into the stitch from which it originally emerged and carry the yarn one stitch to the right to begin another row working downwards.

Second method. This repair is worked over obliquely laid strands and all the freed stitches – plus the corner stitches on both sides of the hole – must be picked up by inserting the needle into each loop and carrying the yarn up and down over the space. Each loop will be picked up twice and the length and number of these strands must correspond to those removed.

Now thread up a slightly finer yarn than used for the main fabric – but in the same color – and make a few stitches in lower left corner to anchor it. Insert the needle upwards into the first loop, pass it under the two strands emerging from the same loop and re-insert it into the same stitch between the two oblique strands, withdrawing it through the next stitch. Continue working into all the loops in this way.

The new loops should be the same size as the existing ones. At the end of the first row, work a few stitches beyond the hole.

Continue as above, turning the work on each row so stitches are always made from left to right.

Repairing purl knitting over oblique strands

The preparatory work must be carried out as for repairing knitting. When the foundation strands have been laid, the oblique strands are then covered by working horizontally: insert the needle to the right of the first two oblique strands emerging from a loop and withdraw it from the left. Continue until all strands are covered. These linking stitches are worked in double rows and set alternatingly.

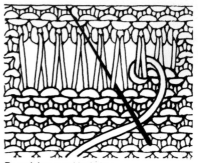

Repairing purl knitting

Repairing single ribbing

The preparatory work must be carried out as described in the two previous examples, with oblique strands. Then proceed by working one stitch as for the knitting repair and one stitch as for the purl knitting repair alternately, in the same order as in the work itself.

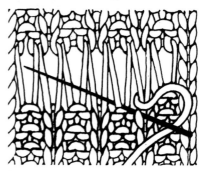

Repairing single rib knitting

Tassels

These can be used very decoratively on berets, scarves, etc.

You will need a piece of cardboard of the same width as the length of tassel you wish to make. Wind the yarn around and around the cardboard. Break the yarn, leaving a few inches free, and thread it through a yarn or darning needle. Slip the needle through all loops at one end of the cardboard and fasten tightly with a knot. Remove cardboard and wind yarn round all the loops, about a quarter of the way down the total length of the tassel from the knot. Draw needle up through the top and fasten off. Now, holding the tassel flat in the left hand, with a sharp pair of scissors cut through all loops at opposite end to fastening and trim.

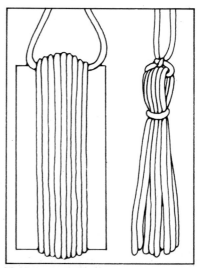

Making a tassel

Pompons

Although pompons are not difficult to make they call for a certain amount of precision but, if well made, can be very decorative. You will need two circles of cardboard, about ¾ in (2 cm) larger in diameter than the pompons will be. Make a hole in the center of both discs about one-fifth the size of the circles and, with a long length of yarn threaded double into a blunt needle, cover the whole disc evenly by taking the needle through the hole and bringing the yarn round and through the hole again. Continue in this way until the center hole is practically closed.

Now, with very sharp scissors, cut around outer edge of circles working between the layers of cardboard as much as possible. Tie a double length of yarn tightly round the center, between the discs, and knot securely. Remove both pieces of cardboard and tidy up the resulting ball with the scissors, making sure that it is as round as possible.

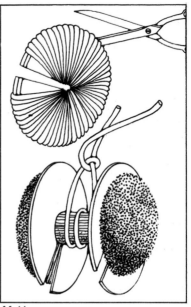

Making a pompon

Simple fringes

Cut a number of strands of yarn into lengths twice as long as the fringe is required to be. Divide them into groups of three or four strands, depending on how thick the fringe is to be and on the bulkiness of the yarn, and fold them in half. With the help of a crochet hook, draw the folded loops of one group through the edge of the border, place all the ends over the hook and draw them through the loops on the hook. Pull up firmly to make a secure – but not tight – knot. Repeat at regular intervals along the edge of the border. Whichever side is chosen, the work must be consistently carried out from the same side. All that remains

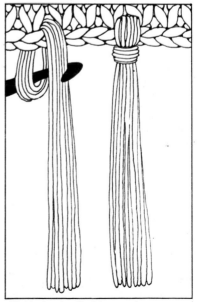

Making a simple fringe

to do is to neaten the edge with sharp scissors – this is best done by laying the fringe flat on a table.

Knotted or lattice fringe

Work as for a simple fringe except that the strands should be cut longer than the fringe is required to be. When all the groups have been knotted into the border, take half the strands of one group and half of the next group and make a knot a short distance down from the first knot. Now knot the remaining strands of the second group to half the strands of the next group and so on to end of fringe. As many rows of knots may be worked as you wish, the knots coming in between the spaces left by the previous line.

Twisted cord

Take a length of yarn about four times the length of cord required. Fold in half and fasten the folded end to a firm surface with a pin. Roll the other end of the two threads between thumb and forefinger until they twist together and begin to curl. Join the end you are holding to the folded end and allow the cord to wind around itself. Fasten the ends together by knotting or stitching, depending upon whether you intend to add a tassel or pompon or fray out the ends.

Simple plaited cord

Take three lengths of yarn about twice the length of cord required. Knot the strands together at one end and fasten to a firm surface with a pin or small tack. Plait in the usual way and secure as already described in previous instruction.

Double plaited cord

Take four lengths of yarn twice the length of cord required. We will call them A, B, C and D. Knot all four strands together at one end and fasten to a firm surface with a pin or small tack. Starting from the left, pass the first strand (A) over the second (B), now pass the third strand (C) under the fourth (D) and over the first (A). The order of the strands, from left to right, will now be B, C, A, D. Once again, pass the first over the second, the third under the fourth and over the first, and so on.

Looped cord

Take a length of yarn eight times the length of cord required and fold it in half. Starting near the fold, make a loop with the forefinger of the right hand and another with the left. Slip the right loop into the left loop from the front, pick up the loop again with the right forefinger and tighten up the left thread by pulling it slightly downwards. Now make another loop on the left forefinger and slip it into the right loop (again from the front). Pick up the loop once more with the left forefinger and tighten up the right thread.

Continue in the same way, alternating from right to left, and always making a new loop on the thread that has just been tightened.

Blocking

This is very important to the success of a knitted article and sometimes it is even possible to remedy slight defects in the work. It is normally advisable to block all the finished pieces of a garment before sewing

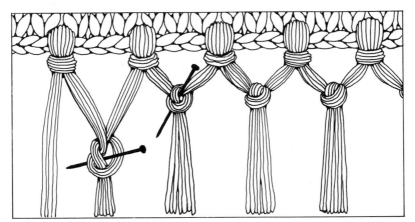

Making a knotted fringe

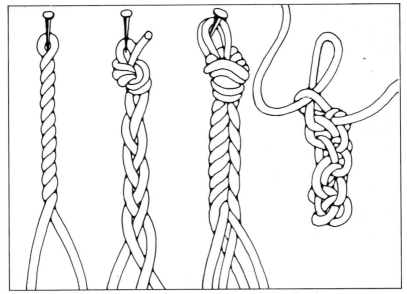

Twisted, simple plaited, double plaited and looped cords

them together. This should be done with steam (either a steam iron or a hot iron over a damp cloth) otherwise a shine may develop and the texture of the knitting be spoiled. In any case it is not advisable to block a raised pattern such as cable stitch except very lightly if there is any distortion; ribbing is never blocked as it would ruin its elasticity.

Block as follows:

1. Pin out the garment pieces wrong side up to the right shape and measurements on a large, flat sur-

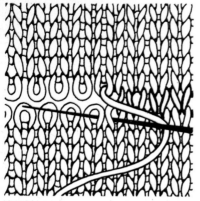

Grafting

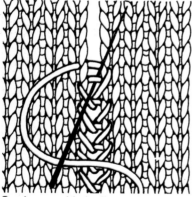

Sewing up with duplicate stitch

Finishing a knitted article

Place the two pieces to be sewn together on top of each other, right sides together. Using a yarn needle, sew along the edges, joining the corresponding stitches of each piece.

Sewing up with duplicate stitch and grafting

Pieces worked in stockinette stitch can be joined almost invisibly in this way. Place the two pieces side by side and, starting from the lower edge, join the first stitch on each side with a needle threaded with the same yarn as the main fabric. Take the needle through the second stitch on the right, withdraw it from the first stitch on the left, insert it under the stitch just made and withdraw.

In the same way, stitches on two edges that have not been bound off can be joined but, of course, in this case, the work is carried out horizontally, thus forming a new row of knitting on the right side. This is called grafting.

By using these two systems of vertical and horizontal sewing, embroidered designs can be worked on garments that have been knitted in stockinette stitch. This is called duplicate stitch.

Decorative sewing up

This method is also carried out. by placing the pieces to be joined side by side. They are joined with a decorative stitch – usually cross-stitch – in a contrasting yarn. This type of embroidery lends itself to simply styled garments and is not suitable for anything which consists of decorative stitches such as raised or openwork designs.

face (over a thick blanket, of course, if a table is used).

2. Place a damp cloth over all the parts to be blocked (omit ribbing).

3. If a steam iron is being used, let it get fairly hot so that there is plenty of steam. If an ordinary iron is being used it should be set at 'cotton'.

4. Pass the iron over the damp cloth, without pressing, to allow the steam to penetrate.

5. Allow the pieces to dry out completely before removing or, if they have to be moved, lay flat on another surface until completely dry.

Imagination and creativity: decorative stitches

BACKGROUND STITCHES

As the heading suggests, the stitches described in this chapter are particularly suitable for fairly heavy garments such as jackets, sweaters, skirts, etc. Whenever a firm textured fabric is required, thick-knit stitches are ideal. They have the great advantage, too, of not being really difficult to do but a little extra care must be taken when a stitch is rather elaborate and each pattern consists of quite a large number of rows. The more decorative the stitch – such as when cabling is involved – the more attention must be paid to accuracy as the least error will spoil the whole design and is hard to rectify.

Stockinette stitch on the bias

1st row: inc 1 st on right side of work at beg of row, k to last 2 sts, k2 tog *.
2nd row: purl.

Twisted stockinette stitch

1st row: k into the back of each st.
2nd row: purl.

Stockinette stitch on the bias

Eightsome stitch

Cast on in multiples of 12 plus an extra 2 sts at each edge for selvedges. (Selvedge sts not included in pat.)

1st, 7th & 13th rows: (wrong side of work) *k1, p2 crossed to the right (purl 2nd st by passing in front of 1st st, purl 1st st) k9 *.

2nd & 8th rows: * p8 k2 crossed right, k2 crossed left (see page 26 for crossing stitches on a knit row).

3rd, 5th, 9th & 11th rows: *p4, k8*.

4th & 10th rows: *p8, k4*.

6th & 12th rows: *p8, k2 crossed left, k2 crossed right, *.

14th & 28th rows: purl.

15th, 21st & 27th rows: *k7, k2 crossed right, k3*.

16th & 22nd rows: *p2, k2 crossed right, k2 crossed left, p6*.

17th, 19th, 23rd & 25th rows: *k6, p4, k2*.

18th & 24th rows: *p2, k4, p6*.

Twisted stockinette stitch

20th & 26th rows: *p2, k2 crossed left, k2 crossed right, p6*.

When 28th row has been worked, repeat from 1st row as required.

Eightsome stitch

Woven basket stitch

Cast on in multiples of 8.
1st row: knit.
2nd and all even numbered rows: purl.
3rd row: k2, *slip 2 sts on to a cable needle and keep to back of work, k2, k2 from cable needle * to last 2 sts, k2.
5th row: *slip 2 sts as if to k on to cable needle and keep in front of work, k2, k2 from cable needle*.
Rep the 3rd and 5th rows alternately.

Woven basket stitch

Chain link stitch

Cast on in multiples of 6.
1st & 3rd rows: *p2, k2, p2*.
2nd and all even numbered rows: k the k sts, and p the p sts, exactly as sts appear on needle.

Chain link stitch

Cherry stitch

5th row: *slip 2 sts as if to p on to a double-pointed cable needle and keep at back of work, k1, p2 from cable needle, slip 1 st on to cable needle and keep in front of work, p2, k1 from cable needle*.
7th row: begin again from the 1st row but changing the position of the 3 st pattern by starting with k1, *p4, k2*.

Cherry stitch

Cherry stitch is worked on the right side of a stockinette stitch background. The 'cherries' should be spaced regularly with 12 stitches (on right side) and 12 rows between them, alternating in the spaces after 1st sequence of cherries has been made.
1st row: *working alternately into front and back, k5 into 1 stitch*.
2nd, 4th & 6th rows: purl.
3rd row: knit.

5th row: slip first 4 sts over the 5th separately, starting with the 4th and working back.
Work 12 rows in stockinette st.
Rep from 1st row.

Sloping cherry stitch

Cast on in multiples of 6.
1st row: *k2, working alternately into front and back, k6 into 1 stitch; now slip 5 of these sts over the 6th (these six stitches make the cherry); p3*.
2nd and all even numbered rows: k the k sts and p the p sts, exactly as sts appear on needle.
3rd row: *p1, k2, 1 cherry, p2*.
As you work, continue moving the pattern 1 st towards the left.

Sloping cherry stitch

Alternating mullion stitch

Cast on in multiples of 6 plus 4.
1st and all odd numbered rows ending with 9th: *k4, p2*, k4.
2nd & all even numbered rows: purl.
11th & all odd numbered rows, ending with the 19th: k1, *p2, k4*, p2, k1.
When 20th row has been worked, rep from 1st row.

Alternating mullion stitch

Reversed mullion stitch

Reversed mullion stitch

1st row: p4, k2.
2nd & all even numberd rows: p the p sts and k the k sts, exactly as sts appear on needle.
3rd & 5th rows: as 1st row.
7th row: p3, *k1, p2, k1, p2*.
9th row: p2, *k1, p4*, k1.
11th, 13th & 15th rows: *k2, p4*.
17th row: as 9th row.
19th row: as 7th row.
When 20th row has been worked, rep from 1st row.

Alternating rib

Cast on in multiples of 10.
1st row: *p3, k1, p3, k3*.
2nd, 3rd & 4th rows: p the p sts, k the k sts, exactly as stitches appear on needle.
5th row: purl.
6th row: * p3, k3, p1, k3*.
Rep these 6 rows as required.

Alternating rib

Rush-mat rib

Rush-mat rib

Cast on in multiples of 19.
1st row: *p5, k2, p5, k1, (k2 crossed right) 3 times*.
2nd row: *p1 (p2 crossed right) 3 times, k5, p2, k5*.

Double rib

Cast on an even number of stitches.
1st row: *k2, p2*.
2nd row: k the k sts, p the p sts, exactly as stitches appear on needle.

English rib

Cast on an even number of stitches.
1st row: knit.

Double rib

English rib

Alternating English rib

2nd row: *k1, k1 in row below (see page 27)*, k2.
Rep the 2nd row, as required.

Alternating English rib

Cast on an even number of stitches.
1st row: knit.
2nd, 3rd, 4th & 5th rows: *k1, k1 in row below (see page 27)*.
6th, 7th, 8th & 9th rows: *k1 in row below, k1*.
When 9th row has been worked, rep 2nd–9th rows, as required.

Mock English rib

Mock English rib

Cast on in multiples of 4.
1st and all odd numbered rows: *k3, p1*.
2nd and all even numbered rows: *k2, p1, k1*.

Wide rib

Wide rib

Cast on in multiples of 7.
1st row: *k5, p2*.
2nd row: k the k sts, p the p sts, exactly as stitches appear on needle.
Rep 2nd row as required.

Sloping rib

Sloping rib

Cast on in multiples of 4.
1st row: *k2, p2*.
2nd, 4th, 6th & 8th rows: work exactly as stitches appear on needle.
3rd row: *k1, p2, k1*.
5th row: *p2, k2*.
7th row: *p1, k2, p1*.
Rep 1st–8th rows as required.

Twisted rib

Wavy rib

Cast on in multiples of 6.
1st, 3rd & 5th rows: *p4, k2*.
2nd, 4th, 6th & 8th rows: k the k sts, p the p sts, as they appear on the needle.
7th row: *p2, slip next 2 sts on to

a cable needle and keep to back of work, k2, p2 from cable needle*.
Maintain p4, k2 ribbing, moving ribs to the right with each cabled pair.

Wavy rib

Reverse rib

Twisted rib

Knit as for single rib but working into the back of each stitch.

Reverse rib

Cast on in multiples of 6.
1st row: (wrong side of work) *k3, p3*.
2nd row: purl
Rep these two rows as required.

Single rib

Single rib

Cast on in multiples of 2.
1st row: *k1, p1*.
2nd row: *p1, k1*.
Rep these two rows as required.

Sylvia's rib

Sylvia's rib

Cast on in multiples of 5.
1st row: *k3, p2*.
2nd row: purl
Rep these two rows as required.

Diagonal rib

Cast on in multiples of 4.
1st row: *k2, p2*.
2nd row: *k1, p2, k1*.
3rd row: *p2, k2*.
4th row: *p1, k2, p1*.
Rep these 4 rows as required.

Broad and narrow rib

Cast on in multiples of 8.
1st and all odd numbered rows: (wrong side of work) *k3, bring yarn to front of work, sl1 purlwise, return yarn to back, k3, p1*.
2nd and all even numbered rows: *k1, p3, k1 into back of st, p3*.
Rep these two rows as required.

Checkerboard stitch

Cast on in multiples of 4.
1st, 3rd & 5th rows: *k4, p4*.
2nd, 4th & 6th rows: work exactly as stitches appear on needle – k the k sts, p the p sts.
7th row: on this row, the pattern is alternated by working 4 p on each 4 k sts and 4 k sts on each 4 p sts of the row before.
8th–12th rows: work exactly as stitches appear on needle.
Rep 1st–12th rows, as required, changing order of purl and knit sts on next and every sixth row.

Diagonal rib

Broad and narrow rib

Checkerboard stitch

Window stitch

Window stitch

Cast on in multiples of 12.
1st, 3rd and 5th rows: *k6, (p2 and then slip both sts on to left needle, take yarn to back of work, return both sts to right needle) 3 times*.
2nd, 4th and 6th rows: purl.
7th, 9th and 11th rows: *(p2, slip to left needle, take yarn to back of work, return sts to right needle) 3 times, k6*.
8th, 10th and 12th rows: purl.
Rep 1st–12th rows, as required, changing pattern order on next and every sixth row.

Floret stitch

Floret stitch

Cast on in multiples of 8 plus 3.
1st, 3rd, 7th, 9th & 11th rows: knit.
2nd and all even numbered rows: purl.
5th row: *k5, work a floret as follows: p3 tog but do not slip them off left needle, knit the

same 3 sts tog, then purl them tog again and slip off needle*. Work from * to * to last 3 sts, k3.
13th row: k3, *k5 and 1 floret*.
Rep from 2nd row.

Flower stitch no 1

A crochet hook will be needed for this stitch.
Cast on in multiples of 8.
1st row: knit.
2nd row: purl.
3rd & 5th rows: *k4, k1 tbl (through back loop), k3*.
4th & 6th rows: *p3, p1 tbl, p4*.
7th row: *k2, insert hook under, over and under horizontal bar that links the 4th st to the twisted k st of 4th row, drawing out a long loop each time and placing each loop on left needle, knit through all 3 loops tog, k2, k1 tbl, k2, insert hook under horizontal bar that links the twisted k st on row 4 to the next st, draw out 3 loops and join them, as above, k1*.
8th row: *p2 tog, p2, p1 tbl, p2, p2 tog, p1*.
9th row: *k4, k4 into next st (working alternately into front and back of st) place these four sts on left needle and p4 tog, k3*.
10th row: purl.
11th row: knit.
12th row: purl.
Rep 3rd–12th rows, as required.

Flower stitch no 2

A crochet hook will be needed for this stitch.
Cast on in multiples of 10.
1st & 3rd rows: *p5, ybk, sl1 as if to p, yfwd, p4*.
2nd & 4th rows: *k4, yfwd, sl1 as if to p, ybk, k5*.
5th row: *p3, k5, p2*.
6th row: *k2, p5, k3*.
7th row: p3 * with hook (pick up right strand of elongated slipped st, yo, draw loop through) twice, yo, draw yarn through both loops and sl this st onto right needle,

Flower stitch no 1

Flower stitch no 2

k5, rep instructions in parentheses for left strand * p2.
8th row: *k2, p2 tog, p3, p2 tog, k3*.
9th row: *p5, k1, p4*.
10th row: knit.
11th & 13th rows: *ybk, sl1 as if to p, p9*.
12th & 14th rows: *k9, yfwd, sl1 as if to p, ybk*.
15th row: *k3, p5, k2*.
16th row: *p2, k5, p3*.
17th row: k3, with hook work second half of pattern as in 7th row *p5, with hook work entire pattern as in 7th row *k2.
18th row: p2, *k5, p2 tog, p3, p2 tog* to last 9 sts, k5, p2 tog, p2.
19th row: *k1, p9*.
20th row: knit.
Rep these 20 rows for pattern.

Flower stitch no 3

Cast on in multiples of 7 plus 2.
1st & 5th rows: *k1, k2 crossed to right, k2 crossed to left (see pages 26-27). Rep to last 2 sts, k2.
2nd row and all even numbered rows: purl.
3rd row: *k2 crossed to right, k2, k2 crossed to left, k1*.
Rep to last 2 sts, k2.
7th row: *k2, sl1 as if to k, k1, psso (pass slipped st over k st), return this st to left needle and k in front and back of it, k3* k2.
9th row: knit.
11th & 15th rows: k2, *k2, k2 crossed right, k2 crossed left, k1*.
13th row: k2, *k1, k2 crossed right, k2, k2 crossed left*.
17th row: k2,* k3, sl1 as if to k,

Flower stitch no 3

k1, psso, return this st to left needle and k in front and back of it, k2*.
19th row: knit.

Gaston's stitch

Cast on in multiples of 8 plus 4.
1st row: knit.
2nd row: purl.
3rd row: *p6, k2*, p2, k2.
4th, 5th & 6th rows: work as stitches appear on needle, k the k sts, p the p sts.
7th row: knit.
8th row: purl.
9th row: p2, k2, *p6, k2*.
10th, 11th & 12th rows: work as stitches appear on needle.
Rep 1st–12th rows, as required.

Gaston's stitch

Seed stitch (moss stitch)

Cast on an uneven number of stitches.
1st row: *k1, p1*.
Next and every following row: rep 1st row, working 1 purl on each knitted stitch and vice versa. Every row will begin and end with k1.

Seed stitch

Double seed stitch (double moss stitch)

1st row: *k1, p1*.
2nd & 4th rows: work exactly as stitches are on needle.
3rd row: *p1, k1*.
Rep these 4 rows as required.

Double seed stitch

Grill stitch

1st row: knit.
2nd row: knit.
3rd row: *k1, p1*.
4th row: work exactly as stitches appear on needle.
Repeat these 4 rows as required.

Grill stitch

Large chain stitch

Large chain stitch

Cast on in multiples of 12.
1st row: *(k1, p1) 3 times, k2, p2, k2*.
2nd row: *p2, k2, p3, k1, p1, k1, p1, k1*.
Continue, working seed st on 6 sts, k2, p2, k2 rib on next 6 sts, for 8 more rows.
11th row: alternate st pattern groups to create link effect: work seed st on rib sts, ribs on seed sts.
Continue 10 rows of pattern, alternating every 11th row.

Plain lozenge stitch

Cast on in multiples of 14.
1st row: *(p1, k1) 4 times, k6*.
2nd and all even numbered rows: work exactly as stitches appear on needle.
3rd row: *(k1, p1) 3 times, k4, p1, k3*.
5th row: *k2, p1, k1, p1, k4, p1, k1, p1, k2*.
7th row: *k3, p1, k4, (p1, k1) 3 times*.
9th row: *k6, (k1, p1) 4 times*.
11th row: as 7th row.
13th row: as 5th row.

15th row: as 3rd row.
16th row: as 2nd row.
These 16 rows form the pattern.

Reversed lozenge stitch

Cast on in multiples of 12.
1st row: *k2, p5, k2, p3*.
2nd and all even numbered rows: work exactly as stitches appear on needle.
3rd row: *p1, k2, p3, k2, p2, k1, p1*.
5th row: *p2, k2, p1, k2, p2, k2, p1*.
7th row: *k1, p2, k3, p2, k2, p1, k1*.
9th row: *k2, p2, k1, p2, k2, p3*.
11th row: *p1, k2, p3, k2, p4*.
13th row: as 9th row.
15th row: as 7th row.
17th row: as 5th row.
19th row: as 3rd row.
20th row: as 2nd row.
These 20 rows form the pattern.

Plain lozenge stitch

Honeycomb stitch

Cast on an even number of stitches.
1st row: knit.
2nd row: knit.
3rd row: *k1, k1 in row below (see page 27).
4th row: *pick up unworked loop from previous row and knit it in with next st, k1*.

Reversed lozenge stitch

5th row: *k1 in row below, k1*.
6th row: *k1, pick up unworked loop from previous row and knit it in with next st.*.
Rep 3rd–6th rows, as required.

Olive stitch

Cast on in multiples of 10 plus 3.
1st row: *k5, p3, k2*. Rep to last 3 sts, k3.
2nd row: p3, *p1, k5, p4*.
3rd row: *k3, p7*. Rep to last 3 sts, k3.
4th row: p3, *k7, p3*.
5th row: *k3, p7*. Rep to last 3 sts, k3.
6th row: p3, *p1, k5, p4*.
7th row: *k5, p3, k2*. Rep to last 3 sts, k3.
8th row: purl.
9th row: *p3, k7*. Rep to last 3 sts, p3.
10th row: k3, *k1, p5, k4*.
11th row: *p5, k3, p2*. Rep to last 3 sts, p3.
12th row: k3, *k2, p3, k5*.
13th row: *p5, k3, p2*. Rep to last 3 sts, p3.
14th row: k3, *k1, p5, k4*.
15th row: *p3, k7*. Rep to last 3 sts, p3.
16th row: purl.
Rep from 1st–16th rows, as required.

Honeycomb stitch

Olive stitch

Wavy stitch

Cast on in multiples of 7.
1st row: knit.
2nd and all even rows: purl.
3rd row: *slip 2 sts onto cable needle and hold them at back of work, k2, k both sts from cable needle, k3*.
5th row: knit.
7th row: *k2, slip 2 sts on to cable needle and bring them to front of work, k2, knit both sts from cable needle, k1*.
9th row: knit.
10th row: purl.
Rep from 3rd–10th rows, as required.

Work 1 extra k st at beg of each odd row and adjust the number of center k st by 2 sts until center of diamond is reached. Center 2 sts should be worked crossed to left. On next odd row reverse direction.
When the pattern of crossed sts has formed a complete diamond, rep from 1st row as required.

Large diamond panel stitch

Cast on in multiples of 16.
1st row: *2 sts crossed to right (k 2nd st on left needle, passing in front of first st, k first st and let both sts slip off left needle), k12*, end 2 sts crossed to left (with right needle behind first st, k into front loop of 2nd st, pull st through behind first st, k first st and pass both sts on to right needle)*.
3rd row: *k1, 2 sts crossed to left, k10, 2 sts crossed to right, k1*.
2nd and all even rows: purl.
5th row: *k2, 2 sts crossed to left, k8, 2 sts crossed to right, *end k2.

Wavy stitch

Large diamond panel stitch

Small mesh stitch

Cast on in multiples of 4 plus 2.
1st row: *k1, bring yarn to front of work and slip 3 sts as if to purl from left to right needle, carry yarn in front of slipped sts and yo around right needle once*. Rep to last 2 sts, k2.
2nd row: purl, allowing the yo st on previous row to drop behind work. (This will produce a bar on right side of work.)
3rd row: knit.
4th row: purl.
5th row: k2, *pick up bar from first row with left needle and knit into the back of it and next st tog, bring yarn to front of work, slip 3 sts as if to purl from left to right needle, carry yarn in front of slipped sts and yo around right needle once*.
6th row: as 2nd row.
7th row: as 3rd row.
8th row: as 4th row.
9th row: k1, *bring yarn to front of work and slip 3 sts as if to purl, carry yarn in front of slipped sts and yo around right needle once, pick up bar from 5th row and knit into the back of it and next st tog,* end k1.
Rep 2nd-9th rows as required.

Ridged diamond stitch

Cast on in multiples of 8.
1st row: *p1, k7*.
2nd row: *k1, p5, k1, p1*.
3rd row: *k2, p1, k3, p1, k1*.
4th row: *p2, k1, p1, k1, p3*.
5th row: *k4, p1, k3*.
6th row: as 4th row.
7th row: as 3rd row.
8th row: as 2nd row.
These 8 rows form the pattern.

Diagonal stitch

Cast on in multiples of 8.
1st row: *p2, k6*.
2nd and all even numbered rows: work exactly as stitches appear on needle.
3rd row: k2, *p2, k6*.
5th row: k4, *p2, k6*.
7th row: *k6, p2*.
8th row: as 2nd row.
Rep 1st–8th rows as required.

Small mesh stitch

Ridged diamond stitch

Embossed diamond stitch

Cast on in multiples of 8.
1st row: *p1, k6, p1*.
2nd and all even rows: work exactly as stitches appear on needle.
3rd row: *k1, p1, k4, p1, k1*.
5th row: *(k2, p1) twice, k2*.
7th & 9th rows: *k3, p2, k3*.
11th row: as 5th row.
13th row: as 3rd row.
15th row: as 1st row.
16th row: as 2nd row.
Rep 1st–16th rows, as required.

Crossed segments stitch

Cast on in multiples of 12 plus 2.
1st row: *k6, p2, k4*. Rep to last 2 sts, k2.
2nd row: p2, *(p2, k2) twice, p4*.
3rd row: *k2, p2, k6, p2*. Rep to last 2 sts, k2.
4th row: k2, *p10, k2*.
5th row: as 3rd row.
6th row: as 2nd row.
Rep 1st–6th rows, as required.

Diagonal stitch

Embossed diamond stitch

Crossed segments stitch

Horizontal segments stitch

Cast on in multiples of 10.
1st row: *k4, p6*.
2nd row: purl.
3rd row: knit.
4th row: purl.
5th row: *p5, k4, p1*.
6th row: purl.
7th row: knit.
8th row: purl.
Rep 1st–8th rows, as required.

Smocking stitch

Cast on in multiples of 6 plus 2.
1st row: p2, *k4 into one st (working alternately into front and back), p2, k1, p2*.
2nd row: *k2, p1, k2, k4 taking yarn round needle twice on each stitch*, k2.
3rd row: p2, *k4 slipping extra loops off needle, p2, k1, p2*.
4th row: as 2nd row.
5th row: as 3rd row.
6th row: *k2, p1, k2, p4 tog*, k2.
7th row: p2, *k1, p2, k4 into one st, p2*.

8th row: *k2, k4 taking yarn round needle twice on each stitch, k2, p1*, k2.

9th row: p2, *k1, p2, k4 slipping extra loops off needle, p2*.

10th row: as 8th row.

11th row: as 9th row.

12th row: *k2, p4 tog, k2 p1*, k2.

Rep 1st–12th rows, as required.

Horizontal segments stitch

Smocking stitch

Herringbone stitch

Herringbone stitch

Cast on in multiples of 28.
1st row: *k6, k2 crossed to right (knit 2nd st on left needle, passing in front of 1st st, then knit 1st st), k2 crossed to left (knit into front of 2nd st going behind 1st st, knit 1st st), k6, k2 crossed to left, k8, k2 crossed to right*.
2nd and all even numbered rows: purl.
3rd row: *k5, k2 crossed to right, k2, k2 crossed to left, k6, k2 crossed to left, k6, k2 crossed to right, k1*.
5th row: *k4, k2 crossed to right, k4, k2 crossed to left, k5, k2 crossed to left, k4, k2 crossed to right, k2*.
7th row: *k3, k2 crossed to right, k6, k2 crossed to left, k6, k2 crossed to left, k2, k2 crossed to right, k3*.
9th row: *k2, k2 crossed to right, k8 k2 crossed to left, k6, k2 crossed to left, k2 crossed to right, k4*.
10th row: purl.
Rep from 1st row, as required.

Rush-matting stitch

Cast on an uneven no of stitches.
1st row: purl.
2nd and all even numbered rows: (right side of work) k1, *sl1 as if to k, k1, yo, pass slipped st over knitted st and new st just made*, k2.
3rd and all odd numbered rows: p1, *sl1 as if to p, p1, yo, psso 2 sts*.
Rep 2nd and 3rd rows as required.

Large rush-matting stitch

Cast on in multiples of 4.
1st row: knit.
2nd row: purl.
3rd row: *k2, slip next 2 sts onto cable needle and keep to back of work, k2, k2 from cable needle*.
4th row: purl.
5th row: *slip 2 sts onto cable needle and keep to front of work, k2, k2 from cable needle*.
6th row: purl.
Rep 3rd–6th rows, as required.

Rush-matting stitch

Woven stitch no 1

Cast on an even number of stitches.
1st row: *k1, yfwd, sl1 as if to p, ybk*.
2nd row: *p1, ybk, sl1 as if to p, yfwd*.
Rep these 2 rows, as required.

Woven stitch no 1

Large rush-matting stitch

Woven stitch no 2

Cast on an even number of stitches.
1st row: *k1, sl1 as if to p, keeping yarn to back of work*.
2nd row: purl.
3rd row: *sl1 as if to p, keeping yarn to back of work, k1*.
4th row: purl.
Rep these 4 rows as required.

sts as follows: *sl2 as if to p, k2*.
6th row: *p2, ybk, sl2 sts as if to k, yfwd*.
Rep from 1st row, as required.

Woven stitch no 3

Cast on in multiples of 4.
1st row: *k2, p2*.
2nd row: *p2, ybk, sl2 as if to k*.
3rd row: *k2, yfwd, sl2 sts as if to p, ybk*.
4th row: *k2, p2*.
5th row: move pattern along by 2

Woven stitch no 2

Woven stitch no 3

Woven rib stitch

Cast on an uneven no of stitches.
1st row: *k1, yfwd, sl1 as if to p,
ybk*, k1.
2nd row: purl.
These 2 rows form pattern.

Diagonal woven stitch

Cast on in multiples of 4.
1st row: *k3, yfwd, sl1 as if to p,
ybk*.
2nd row: purl.
3rd row: *k2, yfwd, sl1 as if to p,
ybk, k1*.
4th row: purl.
5th row: *k1, yfwd, sl1 as if to p,
ybk, k2*.
6th row: purl.
7th row: *yfwd, sl1 as if to p,
ybk, k3*.
8th row: purl.
Rep 1st–8th rows as required.

Woven rib stitch

Diagonal woven stitch

Turban stitch

Twisted cable stitch

Turban stitch

Cast on in multiples of 4.
1st row: *k3, p1*.
2nd row: *p3, k1*.
3rd and all odd numbered rows:
*k 3rd st on needle, going in front
of 1st and 2nd sts, now k 1st st
and pass onto right needle, k 2nd
loop and pass onto right needle
tog with 3rd st already worked;
sl1 as if to p, yo*.
4th and all even numbered rows:

*p3, k tog slipped st and yo from
previous row*.
These last 2 rows form the pattern to be repeated as required.

Twisted cable stitch

Cast on in multiples of 9 plus 3.
1st row: *p3, k6*, p3.
2nd, 3rd & 4th rows: work exactly as sts appear on needle.
5th row: *p3, sl3 sts onto a cable needle and keep to back of work, k3, k3 from cable needle*, p3.
Rep 2nd–5th rows as required.

Alternating cable stitch

Cast on in multiples of 4 plus 2.
1st & 3rd rows: *k2, p2*, k2.
2nd & 4th rows: p2, *k2, p2*.
5th row: *k2 crossed to left, p2* k2 crossed to left.
6th, 8th & 10th rows: work as sts appear on needle.
7th & 9th rows: *p2, k2*, p2.
11th row: *p2, k2 crossed to left*, p2.
12th row: work exactly as sts appear on needle.
Rep these 12 rows as required.

Open cable stitch

Cast on in multiples of 11 plus 3.
1st row: *p3, k8*, p3.
2nd, 3rd & 4th rows: work exactly as sts appear on needle.
5th row: *p3, sl2 sts onto cable

Alternating cable stitch

Open cable stitch

91

needle and hold behind work, k2, k2 sts from cable needle, sl2 sts onto cable needle and hold in front of work, k2, k2 sts from cable needle *p3.
6th–10th rows: work sts as they appear on needle.
Rep 5th–10th rows as required.

3-stitch cable

Cast on in multiples of 9 plus 3.
1st row: *p3, k6*, p3.
2nd row: work exactly as stitches appear on needle.
3rd row: *p3, slip 2 sts onto a cable needle and keep to back of work, k2, k2 from cable needle, k2*, p3.
4th row: as 2nd row.
5th row: *p3, k2, slip 2 sts onto a cable needle and keep to front of work, k2, k2 from cable needle*, p3.
6th row: as 2nd row.
Rep 3rd–6th rows, as required.

3-stitch cable

work, k3, k3 from cable needle) 3 times*, p5.
4th row: as 2nd row.
5th row: as 1st row.
6th row: as 2nd row.
7th row: *p5, k3 (slip 3 sts onto cable needle and keep to front of work, k3, k3 from cable needle) twice, k3*, p5.
8th row: as 2nd row.
9th row: as 1st row.
10th row: as 2nd row.
Rep 3rd–10th rows, as required.

Plaited cable stitch

Cast on in multiples of 23 plus 5.
1st row: *p5, k18*, p5.
2nd row: work exactly as stitches appear on needle.
3rd row: *p5, (slip 3 sts onto a cable needle and keep to back of

Single cable stitch

Cast on in multiples of 7 plus 3.
1st row: *p3, k4*, p3.
2nd, 3rd & 4th rows: work as sts appear on needle.
5th row: *p3, slip 2 sts onto a

Plaited cable stitch

cable needle and keep to back of work, k2, k2 from cable needle*, p3.
6th row: as 2nd row.
7th row: as 1st row.
8th row: as 2nd row.
9th row: as 1st row.
10th row: as 2nd row.
Rep 5th-10th rows, as required.

Single cable stitch

Small cable stitch

Cast on in multiples of 5 plus 3.
1st row: *p3, k2* p3.
2nd, 3rd & 4th rows: work exactly as sts appear on needle.
5th row: *p3, slip 1st st onto a cable needle and keep to back of work, k1, k1 from cable needle*, p3.
Rep 2nd-5th rows, as required.

Small cable stitch

Triangle stitch

Triangle stitch

Cast on in multiples of 12.
1st row: *k6, p1, k5*.
2nd row: *p4, k3, p5*
3rd row: *k4, p5, k3*.
4th row: *p2, k7, p3*.
5th row: *k2, p9, k1*.
6th row: purl.
7th row: *p1, k11*.
8th row: *k1, p9, k2*.
9th row: *p3, k7, p2*.
10th row: *k3, p5, k4*.
11th row: *p5, k3, p4*.
12th row: purl.
Rep 1st-12th rows, as required.

Sloping Tunisian stitch

Horizontal Tunisian stitch

Sloping Tunisian stitch

Cast on any number of sts. Knit first and last sts of each row as selvedge.
1st row: (wrong side of work) *yo, sl1*.
2nd row: *working into backs of sts, k2 tog*.
Rep these 2 rows, as required.

Horizontal Tunisian stitch

Cast on any number of sts. Knit first and last sts of each row as selvedge.
1st row: (wrong side of work) *sl1, yo*. This operation, which is worked on each st, is carried out by slipping 1 st, and taking the yarn right round needle from back to front then slipping the next st, and so on to end of row.
2nd row: *k2 tog, working into backs of new st and slipped st.*

Zara's stitch

Cast on in multiples of 8.
1st row: *p1, k3*.
2nd row: *k1, p5, k1, p1*.
3rd row: *k2, p1, k3, p1, k1*.
4th row: *p2, k1, p1, k1, p3*.
Rep 1st–4th rows, as required.

Zara's stitch

OPENWORK STITCHES AND JACQUARD DESIGNS

Openwork stitches

Openwork stitches require a slightly higher degree of skill than the others; accuracy and evenness of working are vital to achieving an attractive overall appearance. The stitches are usually worked fairly loosely in such a way as to give a soft, light texture, the interwoven designs often being reminiscent of beautiful old lace, giving great scope to the imagination.

These features give an elegance to the work which makes it particularly suitable for the lighter, more delicate garments such as shawls, summer sweaters, evening and lounging clothes, etc. Babies' clothes, too, are delightful when worked in many of these stitches.

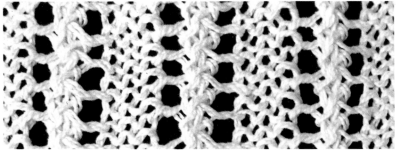

Vertical openwork stitch no 1

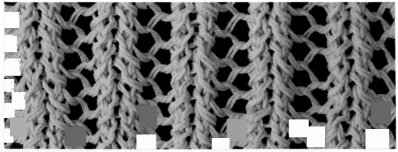

Vertical openwork stitch no 2

Vertical openwork stitch no 1

Cast on in multiples of 6 plus 3.
1st row: *p3, yo, sl1, p2 tog, psso, yrn*, p3.
2nd row: k3, *p3, k3*.
Rep these 2 rows as required.

Vertical openwork stitch no 2

Cast on in multiples of 4.
1st row: *k2, yo, sl1, k1, psso*.
2nd row: *p2, yo, p2 tog*.
Rep these 2 rows as required.

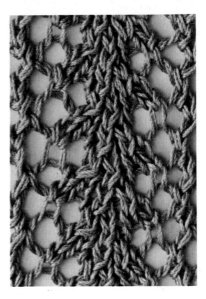

Tree stitch

Tree stitch

Cast on in multiples of 13.
1st row: *(k2 tog, yo) twice, k1, yo, k2 tog twice, k2, yo, k2 tog, yo*.
2nd row: purl.
3rd row: *(yo, k2 tog) twice, yo, k2, k2 tog twice, yo, k1, yo, k2 tog*.
4th row: purl.
Rep these 4 rows, as required.

Wing stitch

Cast on in multiples of 8.
1st row: *p7, k1, yo*.
2nd row: *p2, k7*.
3rd row: *p7, k2, yo*.
4th row: *p3, k7*.
5th row: *p7, k3, yo*.
6th row: *p4, k7*.
7th row: *p7, k4, yo*.
8th row: *p5, k7*.
9th row: *p7, k5, yo*.
10th row: *p6, k7*.
11th row: *p7, k6, yo*.
12th row: *p7, k7*.
13th row: *p7, k5, k2 tog*.
14th row: *p2, tog, p4, k7*.
15th row: *p7, k3, k2 tog*.
16th row: *p2 tog, p2, k7*.

17th row: *p7, k1, k2 tog*.
18th row: *p2 tog, k7*.
19th row: *p3, k1, yo, p4*.
20th row: *k4, p2, k3*.
21st row: *p3, k2, yo, p4*.
22nd row: *k4, p3, k3*.
23rd row: *p3, k3, yo, p4*.
24th row: *k4, p4, k3*.
25th row: *p3, k4, yo, p4*.
26th row: *k4, p5, k3*.
27th row: *p3, k5, yo, p4*.
28th row: *k4, p6, k3*.
29th row: *p3, k6, yo, p4*.
30th row: *k4, p7, k3*.
31st row: *p3, k5, k2 tog, p4*.
32nd row: *k4, p2 tog, p4, k3*.
33rd row: *p3, k3, k2 tog, p4*.
34th row: *k4, p2 tog, p2, k3*.

35th row: *p3, k1, k2 tog, p4*.
36th row: *k4, p2 tog, k3*.
Rep 1st–36th rows, as required.

Horizontal zig-zag stitch

Cast on in multiples of 8 plus 1.
1st row: *k5, yo, k2 tog, k1*, k1.
2nd and all even numbered rows: purl.
3rd row: *k3, k2 tog tbl (through back loop), yo, k1, yo, k2 tog*, k1.
5th row: k1, *k1, k2 tog tbl, yo,

Wing stitch

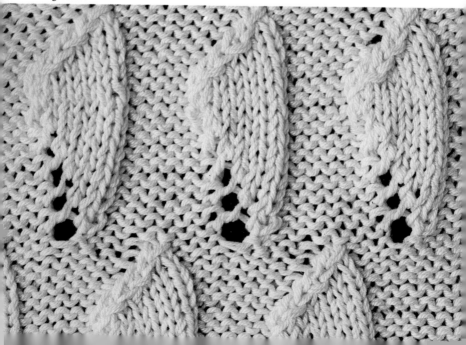

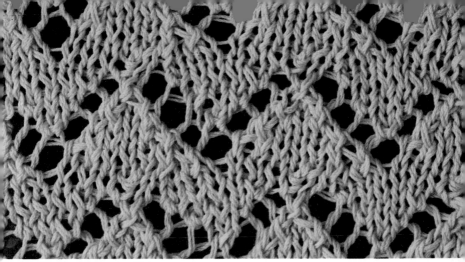

Horizontal zig-zag stitch

k3, yo, k2 tog*.
7th row: *yo, k2 tog tbl, pass st just worked on to left needle and pass next st over it, replace st on to right needle, yo, k5*, k1.
9th row: *k1, k and p into next st, k6*, k1.
11th row: k2 tog, k4, yo, k2 tog, *k2 tog, k5, yo, k2 tog*, k2.
12th row: purl.
Rep 3rd–12th rows, as required.

9th row: *k2 tog tbl, k1, yo*, end k1.
11th row: k1, *k1, *yo, k2 tog tbl*.
13th row: k1, *yo, k2 tog tbl, k1*.
15th row: k1, *k1, yo, k2 tog tbl*.
17th row: *k2 tog tbl, k1, yo*, end k1.
18th row: purl.
Rep 7th–18th rows, as required.

Vertical zig-zag stitch

Cast on in multiples of 6 plus 1.
1st row: k1, *yo, k2 tog tbl (through back loop), k1*.
2nd and all even numbered rows: purl.
3rd row: k1*, k1, yo, k2 tog tbl*.
5th row: *k2 tog tbl, k1, yo*, end k1.
7th row: *yo, sl1, k1, psso, k1*, end k1.

Harebell stitch

Cast on in multiples of 14.
1st row: *p2, k3 tbl, p4, k3 tbl, p2*.
2nd row: *k2, p3, k4, p3 tbl, k2*.
3rd row: *p2, k3 tbl, p4, yo, sl1, k2 tog, psso, yo, p2*.
4th row: *k2, p1, p1 tbl, p1, k4, p3 tbl, k2*.
5th row: as 1st row.
6th row: as 2nd row.
7th row: *p2, yo, sl1, k2 tog, psso, yo, p4, k3 tbl, p2*.
8th row: *k2, p3 tbl, k4, p1, p1 tbl, p1, k2*.
Rep 1st–8th rows, as required.

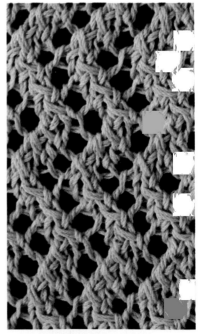

Vertical zig-zag stitch

Open mullion stitch

Cast on in multiples of 6 plus 3.

1st row: p3, *k into horizontal bar between st just worked and next st, p6*.

2nd and all even numbered rows: knit.

3rd, 5th & 7th rows: purl.

9th row: p3, *drop st worked into horizontal bar on 1st row, p3, k into horizontal bar between st just worked and next st, p3*.

11th, 13th & 15th rows: purl.

17th row: *p3, k into horizontal bar between st just worked and next st, p3, drop st worked from horizontal bar on 9th row, p3*.

18th row: knit.

Rep from 3rd row, changing pattern on every 8th row.

Harebell stitch

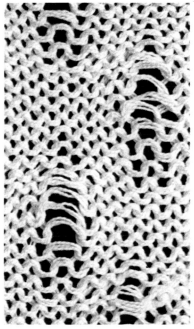

Open mullion stitch

Shell stitch

Shell stitch

Cast on in multiples of 29.
1st row: *k4, sl1, k1, psso, yo, k2, yo, k5, sl1, k2 tog, psso, k5, yo, sl1, k1, psso, yo, k6*.
2nd row: *k4, p2 tog, yo, p3, yo, p4, p3 tog, p4, yo, p1, p2 tog, yo, p2, k4*.
3rd row: *k4, sl1, k1, psso, yo, k4, yo, k3, sl1, k2 tog, psso, k3, yo, k2, sl1, k1, psso, yo, k6*.
4th row: *k4, p2 tog, yo, p5, yo, p2, p3 tog, p2, yo, p3, p2 tog, yo, p2, k4*.
5th row: *k4, sl1, k1, psso, yo, k6, yo, k1, sl1, k2 tog, psso, k1, yo, k4, sl1, k1, psso, yo, k6*.
6th row: *k4, p2 tog, yo, p7, yo, p3 tog, yo, p5, p2 tog, yo, p2, k4*.
These 6 rows complete the pattern. Rep as required.

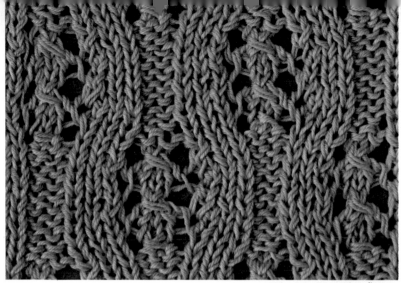

Rib with alternating florets

Rib with alternating florets

Cast on in multiples of 12 plus 3.
1st row: k3, *p3, k3, yo, sl1, k2 tog, psso, yo, k3*.
2nd and all even rows: work exactly as stitches appear on needle.
3rd row: k3, *p3, k3, yo, k3, yo, k3*.
5th row: k3, *p3, k2, k2 tog, yo, sl1, k2 tog, psso, yo, k2 tog, k2*.
7th row: as 3rd row.
9th row: as 5th row.
10th row: as 2nd row.
Rep from 1st row but move the floret design 6 sts to the right to start over the 3 sts previously purled at beg of row and working p3 over floret of previous 10-row repeat.
Alternate position of floret in this manner as required.

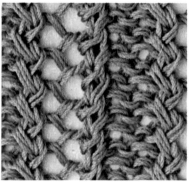

Openwork rib

Openwork rib

Cast on in multiples of 6 plus 2.
1st row: *p2, k2 tog, yo, k2*, p2.
2nd row: k2, *p2 tog, yo, p2, k2*.
Rep these 2 rows, as required.

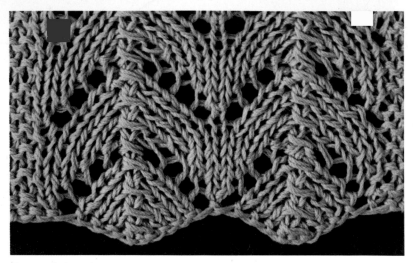

Fancy stitch no 1

Fancy stitch no 1

Cast on in multiples of 10.
1st row: *yo, k3, sl1, k2 tog, psso, k3, yo, k1*.
2nd and all even rows: purl.
3rd row: *k1, yo, k2, sl1, k2 tog, psso, k2, yo, k2*.
5th row: *k2, yo, k1, sl1, k2 tog, psso, k1, yo, k3*.
7th row: *k3, yo, sl1, k2 tog, psso, yo, k4*.
8th row: purl.
Rep 1st–8th rows, as required.

Fancy stitch no 2

Cast on in multiples of 8 plus 3.
1st row: *p3, yo, sl1, k1, psso, k1, k2 tog, yo* end p3.
2nd row: *k3, p5*, end k3.
3rd row: *p3, k1, yo, sl1, k2 tog, psso, yo, k1* end p3.
4th row: as 2nd row.
Rep 1st–4th rows, as required.

Fancy stitch no 3

Cast on in multiples of 5.
1st row: *p1, k1 tbl, p1, yo, k2 tog*.
2nd row: work exactly as sts appear on needle, knitting new st in each pattern.
3rd row: *p1, k1 tbl, p1, k2 tog yo*.
4th row: as 2nd row.
Rep 1st-4th rows as required.

Fancy stitch no 4

Cast on an odd number of stitches.

1st row: k1, *k2 tog*.

2nd row: *k1, yo, pick up horizontal bar linking first to second st and knit, yo*, k1.

3rd row: knit, dropping each 'yo' st but retaining picked-up st. At the end of this row, you should have the same no of sts as originally cast on.

4th row: purl.

Rep 1st-4th rows as required.

Fancy stitch no 4

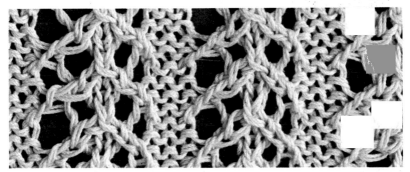

Fancy stitch no 2

Fancy stitch no 3

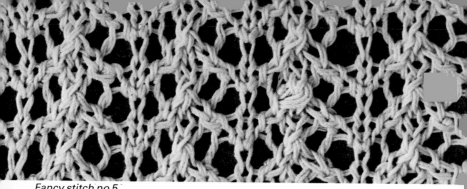

Fancy stitch no 5

Fancy stitch no 6

Fancy stitch no 5

Cast on in multiples of 6 plus 1.
1st row: *k1, yo, sl1, k1, psso, k1, k2 tog, yo*, end k1.
2nd row: purl.
3rd row: *k2, yo, k3 tog, yo, k1*, end k1.
4th row: purl.
These 4 rows form the pattern. Rep as required.

Fancy stitch no 6

Cast on in multiples of 16.
1st row: *k2, yo, sl1, k1, psso, k1, yo, k2 tog, k5, yo, sl1, k1, psso, k2*.
2nd row: *k2, yo, p2 tog, p4, p2 tog, yo, p2, yo, p2 tog, k2*.
3rd row: *k2, yo, sl1, k1, psso, k3, yo, k2 tog, k3, yo, sl1, k1, psso, k2*.

4th row: *k2, yo, p2 tog, p2, p2 tog, yo, p4, yo, p2 tog, k2*.
5th row: k2, yo, sl1, k1, psso, k5, yo, k2 tog, k1, yo, sl1, k1, psso, k2*.
6th row: *k2, yo, p2 tog twice, yo, p6, yo, p2 tog, k2*.
These 6 rows form the pattern. Rep as required.

10th–16th rows: work in stockinette stitch.
Rep these 16 rows, as required.

Butterfly stitch

Cast on in multiples of 10.
1st row: *k2 tog, yo, k1, yo, sl1, k1, psso, k5*.
2nd row: *p7, sl1 as if to purl, p2*.
3rd row: as 1st row.
4th row: as 2nd row.
5th row: knit.
6th row: purl.
7th row: *k5, k2 tog, yo, k1, yo, sl1, k1, psso*.
8th row: *p2, sl1 as if to purl, p7*.
9th row: as 7th row.
10th row: as 8th row.
These 10 rows form the pattern. Rep as required.

Butterfly stitch

Mock polka-dot stitch

Cast on in multiples of 7.
1st row: *k5, yo, p2 tog*.
2nd–8th rows: work in stockinette stitch.
9th row: *yo, p2 tog, k5*.

Mock polka-dot stitch

Open flowery stitch

Cast on in multiples of 12.
1st row: *yo, sl1, k2 tog, psso, yo, k9*.
2nd and all even rows: purl.
3rd row: k3, yo, k2 tog, k5, k2 tog, yo*.
5th row: as 1st row.
7th row: knit.
9th row: *k6, yo, sl1, k2 tog, psso, yo, k3*.
11th row: *k4, k2 tog, yo, k3, yo, k2 tog, k1*.
13th row: as 9th row.
15th row: as 7th row.
16th row: purl.
Rep these 16 rows, as required.

Leaf stitch no 1

Cast on in multiples of 29.
1st row: *k1, sl1, k2 tog, psso, k9, yo, k1, yo, p2, yo, k1, yo, k9, sl1, k2 tog, psso*.
2nd and all even rows: purl.
3rd row: *k1, sl1, k2 tog, psso, k8, yo, k1, yo, k1, p2, k1, yo, k1, yo, k8, sl1, k2 tog, psso*.
5th row: *k1, sl1, k2 tog, psso, k7, yo, k1, yo, k2, p2, k2, yo, k1, yo, k7, sl1, k2 tog, psso*.
7th row: *k1, sl1, k2 tog, psso, k6, yo, k1, yo, k3, p2, k3, yo, k1, yo, k6, sl1, k2 tog, psso*.
9th row: *k1, sl1, k2 tog, psso,

Open flowery stitch

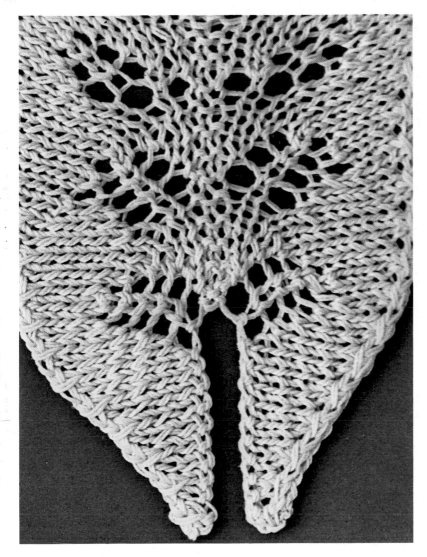

Leaf stitch no 1

k5, yo, k1, yo, k4, p2, k4, yo, k1,
yo, k5, sl1, k2 tog, psso*.
10th row: purl.
Rep these 10 rows as required.

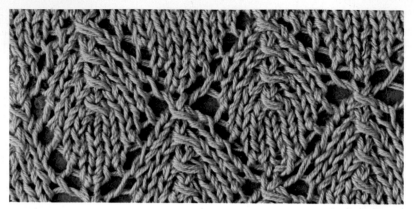

Leaf stitch no 2

Leaf stitch no 2

Cast on in multiples of 10 plus 6.
1st row: k1, yo, *k3, sl1, k2 tog, psso, k3, yo, k1, yo*, k3, sl1, k1, psso.
2nd and all even rows: purl.
3rd row: k2, yo, *k2, sl1, k2 tog, psso, k2, yo, k3, yo*, k2, sl1, k1, psso.
5th row: k3, yo, *k1, sl1, k2 tog, psso, k1, yo, k5, yo*, k1, sl1, k1, psso.
7th row: k4, yo, *sl1, k2 tog, psso, yo, k7, yo*, sl1, k1, psso.
9th row: sl1, k1, psso, k3, yo, *k1, yo, k3, sl1, k2 tog, psso, k3, yo*, k1.
11th row: sl1, k1, psso, k2, yo, k1, *k2, yo, k2, sl1, k2 tog, psso, k2, yo, k1*, k1.
13th row: sl1, k1, psso, k1, yo, k2, *k3, yo, k1, sl1, k2 tog, psso, k1, yo, k2*, k1.
15th row: sl1, k1, psso, yo, k3, *k4, yo, sl1, k2 tog, psso, yo, k3*, k1.
16th row: purl.
These 16 rows form the pattern.
Rep as required.

Leaf stitch no 3

Leaf stitch no 3

Cast on in multiples of 24 plus 2.
1st row: *p2, k6, k3 tog, yo, k1, yo, p2, yo, k1, yo, k3 tog tbl (through back loop), k6*, p2.
2nd and all even rows: *k2, p10*, k2.
3rd row: *p2, k4, k3 tog, k1, yo, k1, yo, k1, p2, k1, yo, k1, yo, k1, k3 tog tbl, k4*, p2.
5th row: *p2, k2, k3 tog, k2, yo, k1, yo, k2, p2, k2, yo, k1, yo, k2, k3 tog tbl, k2*, p2.
7th row: *p2, k3 tog, k3, yo, k1, yo, k3, p2, k3, yo, k1, yo, k3, k3 tog tbl*, p2.
9th, 11th, 13th & 15th rows: work as sts appear on needle.
16th row: as 2nd row.
These 16 rows form the pattern.
Rep as required.

Leaf stitch no 4

Cast on in multiples of 12 plus 6.
1st row: *k1, yo, sl1, k1, psso, k7, k2 tog, yo*, k1, yo, sl1, k1, psso, k3.
2nd and all even rows: purl.
3rd row: *k1, yo, k1, sl1, k1, psso, k5, k2 tog, k1, yo*, k1, yo, k1, sl1, k1, psso, k2.
5th row: *k1, yo, k2, sl1, k1, psso, k3, k2 tog, k2, yo*, k1, yo, k2, sl1, k1, psso, k1.
7th row: *k1, yo, k3, sl1, k1, psso, k1, k2 tog, k3, yo*, k1, yo, k3, sl1, k1, psso.
9th row: *k1, yo, k4, sl1, k2 tog, psso, k4, yo*, k1, yo, k5.
11th row: *k4, k2 tog, yo, k1, yo, sl1, k1, psso, k3*, k4, k2 tog, yo, k1.
13th row: *k3, k2 tog, k1, yo, k1,

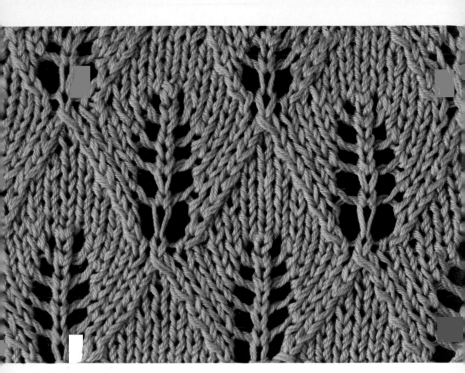

Leaf stitch no 4

yo, k1, sl1, k1, psso, k2*, k3, k2 tog, k1, yo, k1.
15th row: *k2, k2 tog, k2, yo, k1, yo, k2, sl1, k1, psso, k1*, k1, k2 tog, k3, yo, k1.
17th row: *k1, k2 tog, k3, yo, k1, yo, k3, sl1, k1, psso*, k1, k2 tog, k3, yo, k1.
19th row: *sl1, k1, psso, k4, yo, k2 tog, yo, k4*, sl1, k2 tog, psso, k4, yo, k1.
20th row: purl.
These 20 rows form the pattern. Rep as required.

Posy stitch

Cast on in multiples of 10.
1st & 3rd rows: knit.
2nd & 4th rows: purl.
5th row: *insert right needle into 3rd st of 1st row, yo and draw loop through, k2, make 2nd loop in same st as before, k3, make 3rd loop in same st as before, k5*.
6th row: *p5, purl last loop made

(3rd of previous row) tog with next st, p1, purl next loop tog with next st, p1, purl next loop tog with next st*.

7th & 9th rows: knit.

8th & 10th rows: purl.

Rep 5th–10th rows, as required, moving pattern by 5 sts each time sequence is repeated (i.e. start 5th row with k5 and end 6th row with p5 on alternate repeats).

3rd row: as 1st row.

5th row: *k3, yo, sl1, k1, psso, k1, k2 tog, yo*, k3.

7th row: *yo, 1 dbl dec, yo, k1, yo, 1 dbl dec, yo*.

8th row: purl.

These 8 rows form the pattern. Rep as required.

Mosque stitch

Cast on in multiples of 8 plus 3.

1st row: *yo; k2 tog, transfer this stitch back to left needle, pass next st over it, replace st on right needle (1 dbl dec), yo, k5*, yo, 1 dbl dec, yo.

2nd and all even rows: purl.

Posy stitch

Openwork nest stitch

Cast on in multiples of 8 plus 6.
1st & 3rd rows: purl.
2nd row: knit.
4th row: p5, *p1, yfwd, sl 2 sts as if to p, p5*, p1.
5th row: k1, *k5, ybk, sl 2 sts as if to p, k1*, k5.
6th row: p5, *p1, yfwd, sl 2 sts as if to p, p5*, p1.
7th row: k1, *sl1, k1, psso, yo, k2 tog, k1, ybk, sl 2 sts as if to p, k1*, sl1, k1, psso, yo, k2 tog, k1.
8th row: p2, p1, p1 tbl (into made st in previous row), p1, *p1, yfwd, sl 2 sts as if to p, p2, p into back and front of made st in previous row, p1*, p1.
9th row: k1, *k5, ybk, sl 2 sts as if to p, k1*, k5.
10th & 12th rows: knit.
11th row: purl.
13th row: k1, *k1, ybk, sl 2 sts as if to p, k5*, k1, ybk, sl 2 sts as if to p, k2.
14th row: p2, yfwd, sl 2 sts as if to p, p1, *p5, yfwd, sl 2 sts as if

Mosque stitch

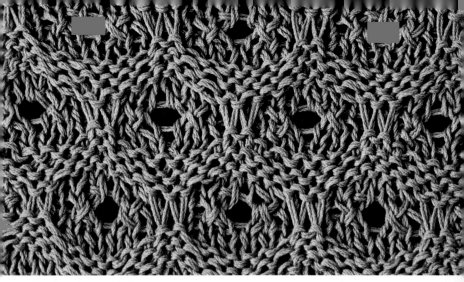

Openwork nest stitch

to p, p1*, p1.

15th row: k1, *k1, ybk, sl 2 sts as if to p, k5*, k1, ybk, sl 2 sts as if to p, k2.

16th row: p2, yfwd, sl 2 sts as if to p, p1, *p2 tog, yo, p1, transfer st to left needle, pick up next st with right needle and pass it over transferred st, replace st on right needle; p1, yfwd, sl 2 sts as if to p, p1*, p1.

17th row: k1, *k1, ybk, sl 2 sts as if to p, k3, k1 tbl (into made st in previous row) k1*, k1, ybk, sl 2 sts as if to p, k2.

18th row: p2, yfwd, sl 2 sts as if to p, p1, *p5, yfwd, sl 2 sts as if to p, p1*, p1.

Rep 1st-18th rows as required.

Ace of spades stitch

Cast on in multiples of 7.

1st row: *k2, k2 tog, yo, k3*.

2nd row: *p1, p2 tog tbl, yo, p1, yo, p2 tog, p1*.

3rd row: *k2 tog, yo, k3, yo, sl1, k1, psso*.

4th row: purl.

5th row: *yo, sl1, k1, psso, k5*.

6th row: *yo, p2 tog, p2, p2 tog tbl, yo, p1*.

7th row: *k2, yo, sl1, k1, psso, k2 tog, yo, k1*.

8th row: purl.

These 8 rows form the pattern. Rep as required.

Pine-cone stitch

Cast on in multiples of 8 plus 2.
1st row: k2, *yo, k2, sl1, k2 tog, psso, k2, yo, k1*.
2nd and all even rows: purl.
3rd row: k2, *yo, k2, sl1, k2 tog, psso, k2, yo, k1*.
5th row: k2, *yo, k2, sl1, k2 tog, psso, k2, yo, k1*.
7th row: k2, *k1, yo, k1, sl1 k2 tog, psso, k1, yo, k2*.
9th row: k2, *k2, yo, sl1, k2 tog, psso, yo, k3*.
11th row: k1, k2 tog, *k2, yo, k1, yo, k2, sl1, k2 tog, psso* to last 7 sts, k2, yo, k1, yo, k2, sl1, k1, psso.
13th row: k1, k2 tog, *k2, yo, k1, yo, k2, sl1, k2 tog, psso* to last 7 sts, k1, yo, k1, yo, k2, sl1, k1, psso.
15th row: k1, k2 tog, *k2, yo, k1, yo, k2, sl1, k2 tog, psso* to last 7 sts, k2, yo, k1, yo, k2, sl1, k1, psso.
17th row: k1, k2 tog, *k1, yo, k3, yo, k1, sl1, k2 tog, psso* to last 7 sts, k1, yo, k3, yo, k1, sl1, k1, psso.
19th row: k1, k2 tog, *yo, k5, yo, sl1, k2 tog, psso* to last 7 sts, yo, k5, yo, sl1, k1, psso.
20th row: purl.
These 20 rows form the pattern. Rep as required.

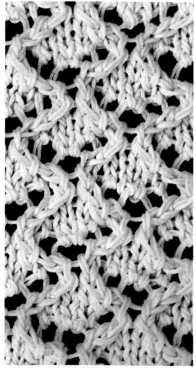

Ace of spades stitch

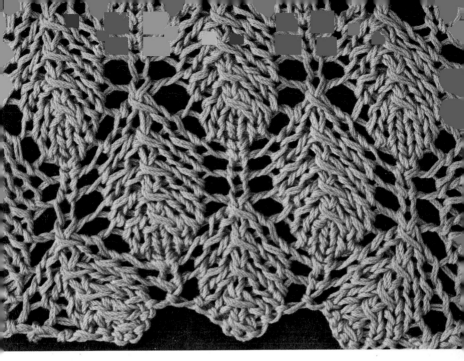

Pine-cone stitch

Lacy stitch no 1

Cast on in multiples of 6 plus 1.
1st row: k1, *yo, sl1, k2 tog, psso, yo, k3*.
2nd row: purl.
3rd row: k1, *k3, yo, sl1 k2 tog, psso, yo*.
4th row: purl.
These 4 rows form the pattern. Rep as required.

Lacy stitch no 2 (Trinity)

Cast on in multiples of 4.
1st row: (wrong side of work): *(k1, p1, k1) into 1st st, p3 tog*.
2nd & 4th rows: purl.
3rd row: *p3 tog, (k1, p1, k1) into next st*.
These 4 rows form the pattern. Rep as required.

Lacy stitch no 3

Cast on in multiples of 4.
1st row: *k2, yo twice, k2*.
2nd row: *p2 tog, k1, p1, p2 tog*.
3rd row: *yo, k4, yo*.
4th row: *p1, p2 tog twice, k1*.
These 4 rows form the pattern. Rep as required.

Lacy stitch no 1

Lacy stitch no 4

Cast on in multiples of 4.
1st row: p2, *yo, p4 tog*, p2.
2nd row: k2, *k1, (k1, p1, k1) into made st of previous row*, k2.
3rd row: knit.
Rep these 3 rows, as required.

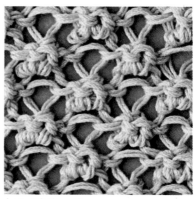

Lacy stitch no 2

Lacy stitch no 3

Mesh stitch no 1

Cast on an even no of stitches.
This pattern consists of 1 row
only: *yo, p2 tog*
Rep as required.

Lacy stitch no 4

Mesh stitch no 2

Cast on an even no of stitches.
This pattern consists of 1 row
only: *yo, sl1, k1, psso*.
Rep as required.

Mesh stitch no 1

Mesh stitch no 3

Cast on in multiples of 5.
1st row: *yo, sl1, k1, psso, k3*.
2nd and all even rows: purl.
3rd row: *k1, yo, sl1 k1, psso, k2
tog, yo*.
5th row: knit.
7th row: *k3, yo, sl1, k1, psso*.
9th row: *yo, k1, yo, sl1, k1,
psso, k2 tog*.
11th row: knit.
12th row: purl.
These 12 rows form the pattern.
Rep as required.

Mesh stitch no 2

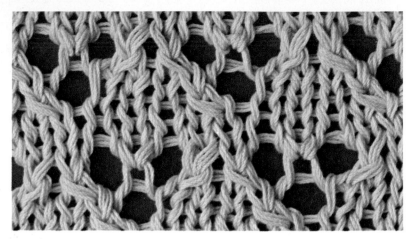

Mesh stitch no 3

Mesh stitch no 4

Cast on an even no of stitches.
1st row: *taking yarn twice around needle, k into 2nd st on left needle, now k into 1st st and slip both sts off left needle*.
2nd row: sl1 st as if to p, *taking yarn twice round needle, k into 2nd st on left needle (i.e. *not* the one made with 2 loops in previous row), p1 into made st and slip all 3 loops off left needle*.
Continue, as required, on these 2 rows, but it must be remembered that each time the 1st row is repeated 3 loops will be slipped off the left needle.

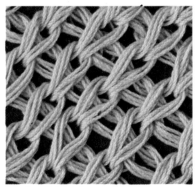

Mesh stitch no 4

Banded openwork stitch no 1

Cast on any number of stitches.
1st–4th rows: knit.
5th row: taking yarn around needle twice for each st, knit.
6th row: purl, allowing 1 loop of each stitch to drop. The effect will be to elongate each stitch.
Rep 3rd–6th rows, as required.

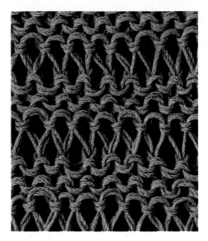

Banded openwork stitch no 1

Banded openwork stitch no 2

Banded openwork stitch no 2

Cast on an even number of stitches.
1st–6th rows: seed stitch (see page 76).
7th row: continuing to work in seed stitch, take yarn around needle twice for each st.
8th row: still retaining seed stitch pattern, allow 1 loop of each stitch to drop as the row is worked.
Rep these 8 rows, as required.

3rd, 5th & 7th rows: *k1, p7*.
8th row: purl.
9th row: *p4, yo, p2 tog, p2*.
10th, 12th & 14th rows: *k3, p1, k4*.

Ladder stitch

Ladder stitch

Cast on in multiples of 8.
1st row: *yo, p2 tog, p6*.
2nd, 4th & 6th rows: *k7, p1*.

11th, 13th & 15th rows: *p4, k1, p3*.
16th row: purl.
These 16 rows form the pattern. Rep as required.

Openwork segments stitch

Cast on in multiples of 9.
1st row: *k7, k2 tog, yo*.
2nd and all even rows: purl.
3rd row: *k6, k2 tog, yo, k1*.
5th row: *k5, k2 tog, yo, k2*.
7th row: *k4, k2 tog, yo, k3*.
9th row: *yo, sl1, k1, psso, k7*.
11th row: *k1, yo, sl1, k1, psso, k6*.
13th row: *k2, yo, sl1, k1, psso, k5*.
15th row: *k3, yo, sl1, k1, psso, k4*.
16th row: purl.
These 16 rows form the pattern. Rep as required.

Openwork segments stitch

Openwork checkerboard stitch

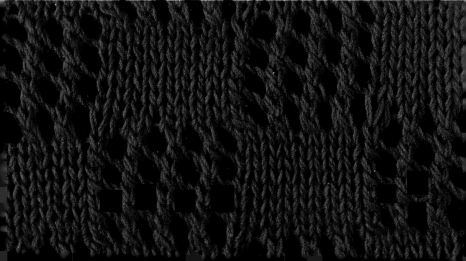

Openwork lozenge stitch

Openwork checkerboard stitch

Cast on in multiples of 16.
1st and all odd rows: (wrong side of work) purl.
2nd, 4th, 6th & 8th rows: *k8, (yo, sl1, k1, psso) 4 times*.
10th, 12th, 14th & 16th rows: *(yo, sl1, k1, psso) 4 times, k8*.

Openwork lozenge stitch

Cast on in multiples of 16.
1st row: *k6, k2 tog, yo, k1, yo, k2 tog, k5*.
2nd and all even rows: knit.
3rd row: *k5, k2 tog, yo, k3, yo, k2 tog, k4*.
5th, 7th, 9th & 11th rows: continue moving the hole-making

sts (k2 tog, yo and vice versa) by one st to left and right on each of these 4 rows (the no of center sts will correspond to row no).

13th row: *k2, yo, k2 tog, k9, k2 tog, yo, k1*.

15th, 17th & 19th rows: continue in pattern but moving hole-making sts by one st to right and left on each of these rows.

20th row: knit.

These 20 rows form the pattern. Rep as required.

Squared openwork stitch

Squared openwork stitch

Cast on in multiples of 8 plus 3.

1st row: knit.
2nd row: purl.
3rd row: *p3, k5*, p3.
4th row: *k2 tog, yo, k1, p5*, k2 tog, yo, k1.
5th row: as 3rd row.
6th row: purl.
7th row: *k4, p3, k1*, k3.

8th row: p3, *p1, k2 tog, yo, k1, p4*.
9th row: as 7th row.
10th row: purl.

Rep 3rd–10th rows as required.

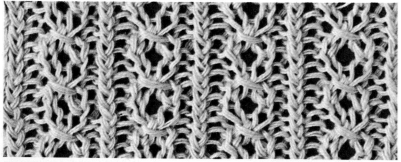

Plaited openwork stitch

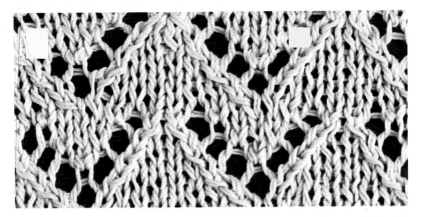

Openwork V-stitch

Plaited openwork stitch

Cast on in multiples of 4 plus 3.
1st row: *p1, k1 tbl (through back loop), p1, k2*, p1, k1 tbl, p1.
2nd row: k1, p1 tbl, k1, *p2, k1, p1 tbl, k1*.
3rd row: *p1, k1 tbl, p1, k1, yo, k1*, p1, k1 tbl, p1.
4th row: k1, p1 tbl, k1, *p3, k1, p1 tbl, k1*.
5th row: *p1, k1 tbl, p1, k3, pick up 3rd st on right needle and slip it over 2 sts.* p1, k1 tbl, p1.
Rep 2nd–5th rows as required.

Openwork V-stitch

Cast on in multiples of 9.
1st row: *k4, yo, sl1, k1, psso, k3*.
2nd and all even rows: purl.
3rd row: *k2, k2 tog, yo, k1, yo, sl1, k1, psso, k2*.
5th row: *k1, k2 tog, yo, k3, yo, sl1, k1, psso, k1*.
7th row: *k2 tog, yo, k5, yo, sl1, k1, psso*.
8th row: purl.
These 8 rows form the pattern.
Rep as required.

Diagonal openwork stitch

Cast on in multiples of 5 (minimum of 10).
1st and all odd rows: knit.
2nd row: *p3, yo, p2 tog*.
4th row: *p4, yo, p2 tog, p4*.
6th row: *p5, yo, p2 tog, p3*.
8th row: *yo, p2 tog, p4, yo, p2 tog, p2*.
10th row: *p1, yo, p2 tog, p4, yo, p2 tog, p1*.
12th row: *p2, yo, p2 tog, p4, yo, p2 tog*.
13th row: knit.
Rep 2nd–13th rows, as required.

Braided openwork stitch

Cast on in multiples of 16.
1st row: *k3, k2 tog, k2, yo, k5, yo, k2, sl1, k1, psso*.

2nd and all even rows: purl.
3rd row: *k2, k2 tog, k2, yo, k1, yo, k2, sl1, k1, psso, k5*.
5th row: *k1, k2 tog, k2, yo, k3, yo, k2, sl1, k1, psso, k4*.
7th row: *k2 tog, k2, yo, k5, yo, k2, sl1, k1, psso, k3*.
9th row: *k5, k2 tog, k2, yo, k1, yo, k2, sl1, k1, psso, k2*.
11th row: *k4, k2 tog, k2, yo, k3, yo, k2, sl1, k1, psso, k1*.
12th row: purl.
These 12 rows form the pattern.
Rep as required.

Triangular openwork stitch

Cast on in multiples of 11 plus 5.
1st row: *k3, (yo, sl1, k1, psso) 4 times* k5.
2nd and all even rows: purl.
3rd row: *k4, (yo, sl1, k1, psso) 3 times, k1*, k5.
5th row: *k5, (yo, sl1, k1, psso)

Diagonal openwork stitch

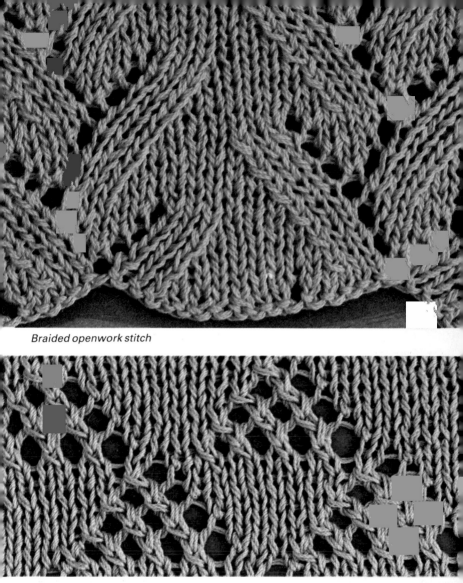

Braided openwork stitch

Triangular openwork stitch

twice, k2*, k5.
7th row: *k6, yo, sl1, k1, psso, k3*, k5.
8th row: purl.
Rep these 8 rows but move

pattern 5 sts on each repeat by working k5 alternately at beg of each row and at end of each row (next sequence will begin with k5).

Sail stitch

Cast on in multiples of 6.
1st row: *p4, yo, k2 tog*.
2nd and all even rows: work as sts appear on needle.
3rd row: *p3, yo, k2 tog, k1*.
5th row: *p2, yo, k2 tog, k2*.

7th row: *p2, k2, k2 tog, pick up horizontal bar between st just worked and next st and purl it*.
9th row: p2, *k1, k2 tog, pick up and p horizontal bar, p4*.
11th row: p2, *k2 tog, pick up and p horizontal bar, p4*.
12th row: knit.
These 12 rows form the pattern.
Rep as required.

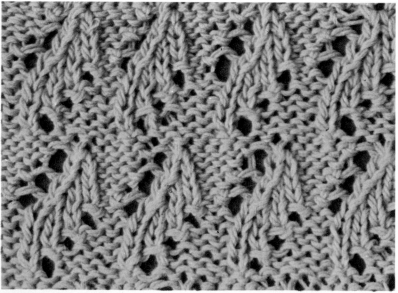

Sail stitch

Fan stitch no 1

Fan stitch no 1

Cast on in multiples of 7 plus 4.
1st row: k2, *yo, sl1, k1, psso, k5*, yo, k2 tog.
2nd and all even rows: purl.
3rd row: k2, *yo, k1, sl1, k1, psso, k4*, yo, k2 tog.

5th row: k2, *yo, k2, sl1, k1, psso, k3*, yo, k2 tog.
7th row: k2, *yo, k3, sl1, k1, psso, k2*, yo, k2 tog.
9th row: k2, *yo, k4, sl1, k1, psso, k1*, yo, k2 tog.
11th row: k2, *yo, k5, sl1, k1, psso*, yo, k2 tog.
12th row: purl.
Rep 1st-12th rows as required.

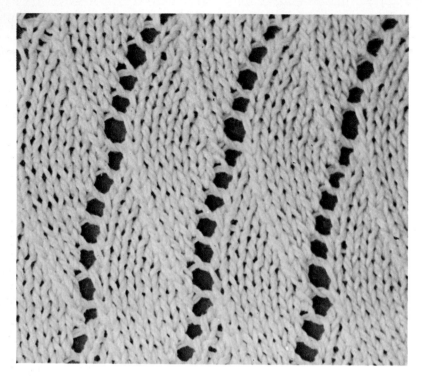

Fan stitch no 2

Fan stitch no 2

Cast on in multiples of 14.
1st row: *k5, sl1, k1, psso, yo, k1, yo, k2 tog, k4*.
2nd and all even rows: purl.
3rd row: *k4, sl1, k1, psso, yo, k3, yo, k2 tog, k3*.
5th row: *k3, sl1, k1, psso, yo, sl1, k1, psso, yo, k1, yo, k2 tog, yo, k2 tog, k2*.

7th row: *k2, sl1, k1, psso, yo, sl1, k1, psso, yo, k3, yo, k2 tog, yo, k2 tog, k1*.
9th row: *k1, sl1, k1, psso, yo, sl1, k1, psso, yo, sl1, k1, psso, yo, k1, yo, k2 tog, yo, k2 tog, yo, k2 tog*.
11th row: k2*, sl1, k1, psso, yo, sl1, k1, psso, yo, k3, yo, k2 tog, yo, k2 tog, k1*.
12th row: purl.
These 12 rows form the pattern.
Rep as required.

Jacquard designs

Jacquard – which includes Fair Isle designs – is always worked in stockinette stitch, the colors being changed according to the chart. The yarns are woven across the wrong side of the work and great care must be taken to maintain an even tension to ensure that these woven yarns neither pull nor sag.

The charts which are given here are used in some of the articles for which instructions are given in the next chapter (pp. 135-250). They are merely suggestions, however; this type of work gives great scope to the imagination. Almost any creative designs can be worked out to decorate knitwear, according to personal taste. These may be worked in one contrasting colour only or in several.

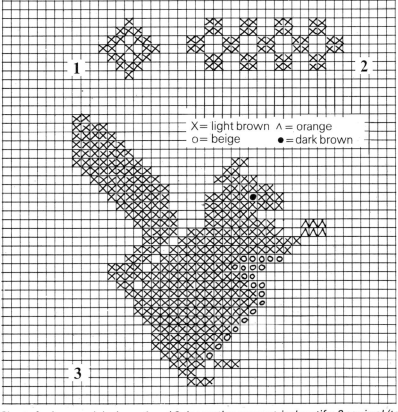

X= light brown ∧ = orange
o= beige ●=dark brown

Charts for jacquard designs: 1 and 2 decorative geometrical motifs; 3 squirrel (to use see pages 160-1 and 198-9 respectively).

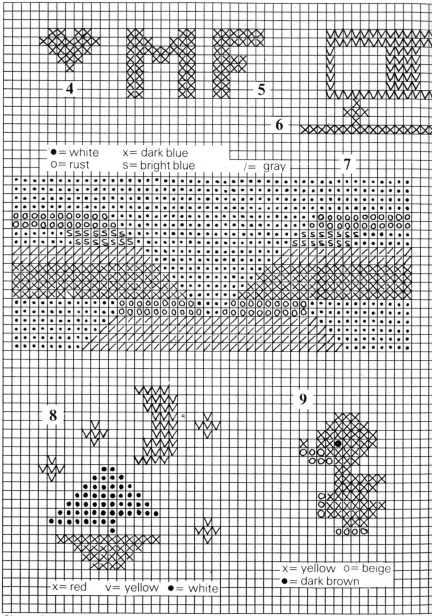

● = white   x = dark blue
o = rust   s = bright blue   / = gray

x = yellow   o = beige
● = dark brown

x = red   v = yellow   ● = white

Charts for jacquard designs: 4 heart; 5 initials; 6 train; 7 decorative pattern; 8 seascape; 9 duckling; 10 geometrical design; 11 snowflake; 12 Greek pattern (to

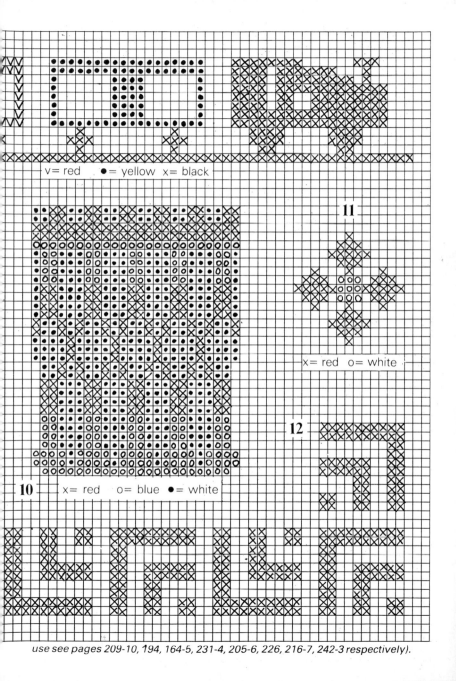

v= red   ●= yellow   x= black

11

x= red   o= white

12

10   x= red   o= blue   ●= white

use see pages 209-10, 194, 164-5, 231-4, 205-6, 226, 216-7, 242-3 respectively).

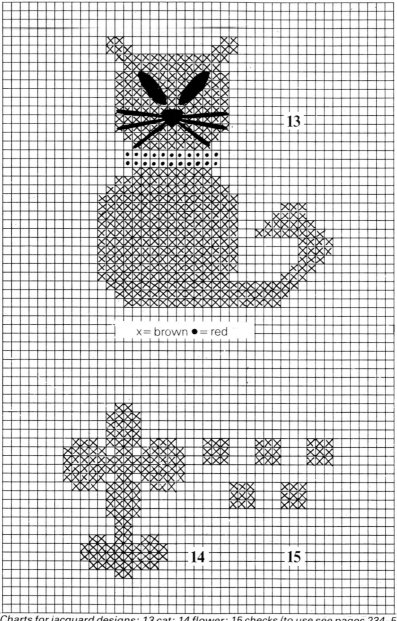

x= brown ● = red

13

14　　15

Charts for jacquard designs: 13 cat; 14 flower; 15 checks (to use see pages 234–5, 212–3 respectively).

Putting it all into practice: standard patterns

The following projects are not intended as fully detailed, sized patterns but, rather, are examples of ways in which the stitches and techniques you have learned in the first part of the book can be utilized. All the projects for adults are made in a medium size range. However, you will need to take your choice of yarn and needles and make a swatch in the pattern stitch. When you have your gauge, you will need to adjust the number of stitches as necessary for the measurements of the size you require.

KNITTED THINGS TO WEAR

Patterns for women

All – or nearly all – women's clothes can be knitted, whether it be a bedjacket or a skirt, an overcoat or a jacket, a casual sweater or an elegant classic pullover.

In the instructions that follow, our aim has been merely to give basic details – shapes, colors and even new designs are yours to maneuver as you will, to your own taste and style.

Off-white overcoat

Materials: 16 skeins (3½ oz/100 gr) natural wool worsted weight (Aran type); 1 pair of no 6 needles; 5 buttons (bone, if possible); 1 buckle. Stitches used: reversed stockinette stitch (purl side is right side), single rib (see page 69).

Back: (worked in 2 pieces) cast on 70 sts. Work in reverse st st for 35½ ins (90 cm), at the same time decreasing gradually one side only until there are 42 sts on needle. Continue working straight for another 12 ins (30 cm). Bind off. Work a second piece to match (i.e. with decs on opposite side).

Front half: cast on 80 sts and work in reverse stockinette st for 36½ ins (93 cm), decreasing gradually at both sides until there are 51 sts on needle. Remember that an internal vertical pocket is to be started when 24½ ins (62 cm) have been worked (see page 43), the opening to be 6½ ins (16 cm) deep.

Continue without shaping for a further 6 ins (15 cm) then dec 1 st 18 times at neck edge. Work another 4 ins (10 cm) without shaping. Bind off.

Work second half to match, reversing shapings.

Sleeves: cast on 70 sts and work in reverse st st for 24 ins (60 cm). Continue, increasing 4 sts on both sides, until work measures 27½ ins (70 cm). Bind off.

Finishing: sew sides and back together and join shoulders. Sew sleeve seams and insert sleeves into armholes. Pick up the neck stitches evenly and work in single rib for 7 ins (18 cm). Bind off.

Starting from lower edge, pick up all the stitches of left front edge, including the edge of collar just worked. Work in single rib (k1 p1) for 2 ins (5 cm). Bind off fairly loosely. Work right front edge to match, picking up the same number of stitches, but work 5 horizontal buttonholes (see page 40), evenly spaced, starting about 13¾ ins (35 cm) from lower edge.

For hem, turn up about 2¾ ins (7 cm) and sew neatly in place.

For cuffs, fold back about 3 ins (8 cm), twice, and hold in place with a few stitches at seam and opposite side.

For pocket welts, pick up stitches along pocket edge and work in single

Off-white overcoat

rib for 2 ins (5 cm). Work second welt to match.

Belt: using tubular method (see page 20), cast on 10 sts and work for 47 ins (120 cm). Make 2 more lengths in the same way. Plait the 3 lengths, fasten each end with a few stitches and sew on buckle.

Sew buttons into place, matching their positions to the buttonholes.

Light brown coat

Materials: 18 skeins (3½ oz/100 gr) worsted weight yarn, worked double; 1 pr of no 10 needles; cable needle; 5 buttons.

Stitches used: garter stitch, stockinette stitch, single cable stitch (see page 92).

Back: cast on 70 sts and work 4 ins (10 cm) in garter st. Change to st st and work 25½ ins (64 cm). Begin armhole shaping by decreasing 2 sts on each side until 56 sts remain, ending on wrong side of work.

Next row: (right side of work) p2, k4, p2, k4, p6, k4, p2, k4, p6, k4, p2, k4, p6, k4, p2.

On next and alt rows: work exactly as stitches are on needle.

On rows worked on right side of work, continue in single cable st on each k4, keeping purl insertions exactly as instructed above. The cables should be crossed alternately left and right, i.e. on the 4 sts each side of a 'p2', the first is worked to the left and the second to the right. Continue in this way for 10 ins (25 cm). Bind off.

Left front: cast on 50 sts and work 4 ins (10 cm) in garter st. Change to st st, but knit the first 10 sts of each purl row to create the garter st border, and the 11th–16th sts (on right side rows) and the 34th–40th sts (on wrong side rows) in single cable, starting as follows: k4 (these are the sts to be cabled), p2. The return rows, worked on the wrong side, will therefore end with: k2, p4, k10. Continue in this way for 25½ ins (65 cm). Begin armhole shaping by decreasing 2 sts at armhole edge until 48 sts remain, ending on wrong side of work.

Next row: (right side of work) garter st 10, k4, p2, k4, p6, k4, p2, k4, p6, k4, p2. Continue as for back (working single cable st on each k4), for 10 ins (25 cm). Bind off.

Right front: work as for left front but keep garter st border, cable insertion and armhole decreasing on opposite side. When the work measures nearly 23 ins (58 cm), work the first vertical buttonhole (see page 40) in garter st border. As work progresses, make 4 more buttonholes 3½ ins (9 cm) apart.

Sleeves: these are worked lengthwise. Cast on 76 sts.

1st row: k10 (cuff), p2, k4, p6, k4, p2, k4, p6, k4, p2, k4, p6, k4, p2, k4, p6, k4, p2. On each k4, work single cable st as before.

On next and alternate rows, work exactly as stitches appear on needle except for last 10 sts which will be knitted, as the cuff is in garter st.

Continue straight for 15¾ ins (40 cm). Bind off.

Cowl collar: cast on 81 sts.

1st row: k10, p2, k4, p2, k49, p2, k4, p2, k10. On each k4, work single cable st, as before.

On next and alternate rows, work exactly as stitches appear on needle except for first and last 10 sts which will be knitted to form a garter st border on both sides.

Continue for nearly 8 ins (20 cm) ending on the wrong side. Continue in pattern but dec 1 st each side of

138

Navy blue jacket

center st of st st panel on next and every alternate row 15 times (39 sts). Bind off.

Pockets (make 2): Cast on 30 sts.
1st row: k10, p2, k4, p2, k4, p8. Work single cable st on each k4 as before.

Next and alternate rows: work ex- actly as sts appear on needle, except for last 10 sts which are knitted to form garter st border.

Finishing: sew back and front sides together and shoulder seams; sew sleeve seams and set sleeves into armholes. Attach cowl collar but, before doing so, ensure that it is centered by folding in half and marking center point on one side with a pin; mark center back of coat in a similar way and join the two markers; sew neatly with a flat seam so that garter st borders continue in line with front borders of coat. Mark positions for patch-pockets and sew in place. Sew on buttons to match buttonholes.

Navy blue jacket

Materials: 20 skeins (1¾ oz/50 gr) fingering weight yarn; 1 pr no 6 needles; 1 pr no 1 needles; 3 buttons.
Stitch used: single rib (see page 69).
Back: with no 6 needles and using the tubular method, cast on 120 sts. Work 29½ ins (75 cm) in k1 p1 rib. Bind off.
Left front: cast on 84 sts (tubular method). Work 27½ ins (70 cm) ending on wrong side of work. Bind off 26 sts for neckline shaping and continue decreasing 1 st at neck edge on right side of work only until work measures the same as the back.
Right front: work in the same way, reversing neck shaping and working 2 double vertical buttonholes (see page 40) at equal distances from about two-thirds of the way up.
   The front facings are formed by turning in 14 sts or 2 ins (5 cm) on both front edges. These should be neatly stitched in place so that the double buttonholes are properly in position, the buttonhole on the outside corresponding to its counterpart in the facing. Work round each buttonhole in buttonhole stitch, joining front and facing together.
Sleeves (work 2): cast on 132 sts. Work 25½ ins (65 cm) in single rib. Bind off.
Pockets (work 2): cast on 52 sts.

Work 7¾ ins (20 cm) in single rib. Bind off.
Finishing: join fronts and back at sides; join shoulders; join sleeve seams and set sleeves in. Position patch-pockets and sew neatly into place.
Neckband: with no 1 needles, cast on 140 sts and work in single rib for ¾ ins (2 cm). Now make a double vertical buttonhole near one end of the strip (at the same distance from the edge as the buttonholes already worked on jacket front). Continue in single rib until work measures 4 ins (10 cm). Bind off.
   Fold this strip in half lengthwise, make a closed tube of it by sewing both ends together and long edges. Mark center and also center back of neck edge; join these two markers, pin neckband in position and sew neatly in place, ensuring that buttonhole comes on right front. Neaten buttonhole and sew on buttons.

White jacket

Materials: 8 skeins (3½ oz/100 gr) worsted weight yarn; 1 pr no 10½ needles; cable needle; 4 buttons.

Stitches used: garter stitch, stockinette stitch, single rib (see page 69), double rib (see page 66), triple (tr) rib (k3 p3).

Back: cast on 48 sts. Work 1½ ins (4 cm) in garter st. Now, keeping the first and last 15 sts in triple rib, continue in diamond cable pattern as follows:

Next row: (right side of work) tr rib for 15 sts, k2, p5, slip next 2 sts onto cable needle and keep at front of work, k2, knit both sts from cable needle, p5, k2, tr rib for 15 sts.

2nd and all even rows: beg and end each row with tr rib; work the 18 sts between as they appear on needle.

3rd row: tr rib for 15 sts, k2, p4, slip next st onto cable needle and keep at back of work, k2, purl st from spare needle, slip next 2 sts onto cable needle and keep at front of work, p1, k both sts from cable needle, p4, k2, tr rib for 15 sts.

5th–9th rows: keeping tr rib border of 15 sts at each end of row, continue working odd numbered rows as instructed, decreasing by 1 the no of purl sts worked after the first 17 sts and before the last 17 sts (i.e. thus keeping tr rib borders plus k2), to form the diamond shape.

11th–17th rows: work as before but increasing the no of purl sts worked at each end of panel until there are 5 purl sts. When 18th row has been worked, repeat from 1st row. Continue for 13¾ ins (35 cm), keeping borders in tr rib and retaining central diamond panel pattern. Now start shaping for raglan armhole (see page 45), working 2 sts in st st at each end of every row. Continue until work measures 9½ ins (24 cm) from beg of shaping. Bind off.

Right front: cast on 29 sts. Work 1½ ins (4 cm) in garter st, ending on right side of work.

Now, keeping the first 6 sts in tr rib and the last 5 sts in garter st (center front border) on each row, work the center 18 sts in diamond cable exactly as for back. Make 4 horizontal buttonholes at regular intervals (see page 40) in garter st border. On completion of 1st diamond, work an incorporated horizontal pocket (see page 41) with 1½ in (4 cm) border in single rib. Continue until work measures 13¾ ins (35cm), keeping center border in garter stitch and side edging of 6 tr rib. Now start shaping for raglan armhole as for back, at the same time increasing the garter stitch border at center front by 1 st on next 18 rows (23 sts now in garter st border).

When work measures the same as back, slip garter st border onto a spare needle and bind off remaining stitches. Replace sts from spare needle to one of the main needles and continue in garter st for half the width of the sts cast off at neck on back.

Left front: work as for right front, reversing shaping and omitting buttonholes.

Sleeves: (make 2) cast on 24 sts. Work 2¾ ins (7 cm) in single rib. Continue for 15 ins (38 cm) in double rib increasing 1 st at both ends of every 8th row (right side of work). Now start raglan shaping (see page 45) and continue until armhole measures the same as back armhole.

Finishing: sew front and back side seams together. Sew sleeve seams and stitch into place along sloping shoulder lines with a flat seam. Join backs of collar and stitch collar into place, being careful to center the joint at center back. Sew on buttons.

White jacket

Light brown jacket

Materials: 7 skeins (3½ oz/100 gr) worsted weight yarn in light brown; 1 pr of no 9 needles; 4 buttons.
Stitches used: stockinette stitch, seed stitch (see page 76).
Back: cast on 58 sts. Work 2½ ins (6 cm) in seed st and then change to st st, shaping for waist by decreasing 1 st at both ends of every 10th row 3 times. Continue on these 52 sts until work measures 15¾ ins (40 cm) from the start, ending on wrong side.

For armhole shaping, bind off 3 sts at beg of next 2 rows and then dec 1

Light brown jacket

144

st at beg of foll 2 rows. Continue in st st and when armhole measures 8¼ ins (21 cm), work neck shaping as follows: k14, bind off 16 sts, k14. Next row: bind off 7 sts, p7. Next row: bind off rem 7 sts. Break yarn and fasten off. Transfer rem 14 sts onto second needle, join yarn and bind off 7 sts, k7. Next row: bind off rem 7 sts. Break yarn and fasten off.

Left front: cast on 44 sts. Work 2½ ins (6 cm) in seed st. Starting from side edge, begin to introduce st st, increasing st st pattern by 1 st on every row (thus decreasing the seed st pattern at the same time) until 5 sts remain in seed st. (These will be retained to form center front border.)

At the same time, dec 1 st every 10 rows 3 times at side edge.

Continue until work measures the same as back at armhole shaping. Bind off 3 sts on next row at side edge and 1 st on foll row.

When work measures 19¾ ins (50 cm) from beginning, bind off the 5 seed sts and continue in st st, decreasing 1 st on every row at neck edge on right side of work until 14 sts remain. Bind off in 2 groups of 7 sts, starting from outer shoulder edge.

Right front: work as for left front, reversing pattern and shaping. Make 4 buttonholes, the first one just over 7¾ ins (20 cm) from lower edge and the other three at 4 ins (10 cm) intervals.

Sleeves: (make 2) cast on 31 sts. Work 12 rows in seed st. Now introduce st st at each end of row, starting with 1 st and increasing st st pattern by 1 st on each row (thus decreasing the seed st pattern at the same time) until the seed st is reduced to 1 purl st on the st st. Continue in st st, increasing 1 st at each end of every 8th row. When work measures 15¾ ins (40 cm) from beginning, bind off 4 sts at beg

of next 2 rows and then dec 1 st at each end of every knit row until 22 sts remain. Bind off.

Half collar: (make 2) cast on 22 sts. Work in seed st for 10¼ ins (26 cm), then dec 1st at one end of every row on right side of work until 1 st remains. Fasten off. Work 2nd piece in the same way.

Finishing: sew up side seams and shoulders. Join sleeve seams and set sleeves into armholes. Join (with flat seam) center seam of collar and stitch collar in place, being careful to keep center collar seam to center back. Sew on buttons.

White jacket and hood in chenille

Materials: 2 skeins (3½ oz/100 gr) long-fibered white chenille; 5 skeins short-fibered white chenille; 1 pr each of nos 9 and 11 needles; 4 white hooks (as used by furriers).

Stitches used: garter stitch, stockinette stitch.

The back and 2 fronts are worked in one piece.

Cast on sts to measure 47¼ ins (120 cm) with the short-fibered chenille. Work 4 ins (10 cm) in st st. Make 2 incorporated vertical pockets (see page 43) 6 ins (15 cm) from lower to top edges, set 12 ins (30 cm) in from the edges of the work – the pockets will be positioned exactly at the sides of the jacket. Continue in st st for nearly 10 ins (25 cm) decreasing 1 st every 3 rows, on right hand side of work, in line with pockets (i.e. at each side of jacket).

For armholes, bind off 4 sts for each armhole – 2 sts on each side of line from pockets. From now on, the work will be continued in 3 sections. Work as follows on each piece: 6 ins (15 cm) in st st, then dec 1 st at neck edge of fronts on every row on right side of work for another 2¾ ins

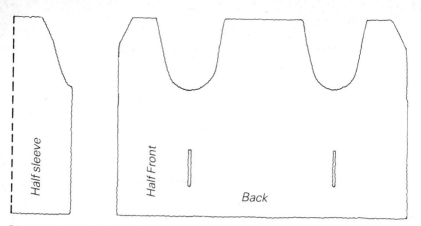

Diagram for white jacket in chenille

(7cm). Bind off.

Sleeves: (make 2) cast on sts to measure 12 ins (30 cm). Work 13¾ ins (35 cm) in st st. For armhole shaping, bind off 2 sts at beg of next 2 rows and then continue in st st, decreasing 1 st at both ends of the row, on right side of work, for 4¾ ins (12 cm). Bind off.

Finishing: stitch up shoulder seams. Join sleeve seams and set sleeves into armholes. Pick up the stitches around the wrist and with the long-fibered chenille work 2¼ ins (6 cm) in garter st. Work second cuff to match.

Pick up all the stitches along lower edge of jacket and with the long chenille work in garter st for 3¼ ins (8 cm). Pick up the sts down each center front and neck opening with the same chenille and work in garter st for 3¼ ins (8 cm). Sew on hooks at regular intervals.

Hood. Materials: 1 skein (3½ oz/100 gr) long-fibered white chenille; 1 pr of no 11 needles.

Stitch used: garter stitch.

Cast on sts to measure 7¾ ins (30 cm). Work 19¾ ins (50 cm) in garter st. Bind off. Fold in half lengthwise

and join back seam. Sew a 12 ins (30 cm) length of chenille to each free corner as ties.

Blue polo-neck sweater

Materials: 12 skeins (1¾ oz/50 gr) mohair 2-ply; 1 pr each of nos 1 and 2 needles; 1 set of 4 no 2 double-pointed needles.

Stitches used: single rib (see page 69), English rib (see page 66), twisted rib (see page 69).

Back: cast on 84 sts. With no 1 needles work 2⅜ ins (6 cm) in single rib. Change to no 2 needles and work 2⅜ ins (6 cm) in English rib, then in twisted rib for 3½ ins (9 cm), English rib for 4¾ ins (12 cm) and twisted rib for 2 ins (5 cm). Continue in twisted rib, shaping for raglan shoulder by decreasing 1 st at each end of every row on right side of work, for 1½ ins (4 cm). Continuing to decrease as before, work in English rib for 5 ins (13 cm). Bind off.

Front: work as for back until front measures 2 ins (5 cm) shorter than back. Make neck opening by binding off center 10 sts. Work each shoul-

HOW TO KNIT BEDROOM SLIPPERS

USING GENUINE LAMBS WOOL SOLES

Cast on 6 stitches — then knit 1 row plain to make a firm edge.

1. Knit 2, make 1 (by putting the wool around the needle), knit 2, pass the made stitch over the 2 knitted ones and let it slip down, knit 2, cast on 2.

2. (Knit 2, purl 2) twice, cast on 2.

3. Make 1, knit 2, pass the made stitch over, *knit 2, make 1, knit 2, pass the made stitch over; repeat fro *once, cast on 2.

4. Purl 2, knit 2; repeat twice, cast on 2.

5. Knit 2, *make 1, knit 2, pass the made stitch over, knit 2; repeat from *twice on 2.

6. Knit 2, purl 2, repeat, and cast on 2 at the end.

7. Make 1, knit 2, pass the made stitch over, *knit 2, make 1, knit 2, pass the made stitch over; repeat from * to the end of the row, cast on 2.

8. Purl 2, knit 2; repeat to the end of the row, cast on 2.

9. Knit 2, * make 1, knit 2, pass the made stitch over, knit 2; repeat from * to the end of the row; cast on 2.

10. Knit 2, purl 2; repeat to the end of the row, cast on 2.

Repeat the last 4 rows until there are 54 stitches. Then work without increasing for 15 rows. The last row will be a pattern row.

NEXT ROW. Work 18 stitches as usual, cast off 18, work to the end of the row as usual. Work on these last 18 stitches in the pattern until the strip is long enough to reach to the back of the heel, the number of rows depending upon the size required. Bind off these stitches.

Begin again where you divided and work the other 18 stitches in the same way, and cast them off when they reach the heel.

Holding the work with the right side toward you, take the wool of contrasting color and pick up and knit the stitches all around the top of the slipper, beginning at one side of the heel, and continuing all around to the other side.

Work 1 row purl and 1 row plain alternately for 14 rows. Bind off loosely — this will form a roll around the top of the slipper.

Join up the heel of the slipper and the back of the roll. Sew to the sole and trim with a pompon.

Manufactured by

STUART MFG. CO.   Paterson, N. J.

White jacket and hood in chenille

der piece separately to match back.
Sleeves: with no 1 needles, cast on
45 sts. Work in single rib for 3⅛ ins
(8 cm). With no 2 needles, continue
in English rib for 2⅜ ins (6 cm)
twice increasing 1 st at each edge on
right side of work. Continue in

twisted rib for 4 ins (10 cm), twice
increasing 1 st at each edge on right
side of work. Continue for 6 ins (15
cm), repeating the increases, then
work 2 ins (5 cm) in twisted rib. Now
begin to decrease for raglan shaping
(see page 45) and work in the same

147

Blue polo-neck sweater

stitch for 2 ins (5 cm), then in English rib, still decreasing, for 5½ ins (14 cm). Bind off. Work second sleeve in exactly the same way.

Finishing: sew sides together, join sleeve seams and set sleeves into position. With the 4 double-pointed needles, pick up all stitches evenly round the neck opening and work in twisted rib for 11 ins (28 cm). Bind off. When binding off around the neck it is important to make the tension just right – neither too tight nor too loose.

Mauve pullover

Materials: 12 skeins (1¾ oz/50 gr) 4-ply mohair; 1 pr of no 7 needles and 2 spare needles in same size; 1 no H/ 8 crochet hook.

Stitches used: double rib (see page 66), stockinette stitch.

Back: cast on 50 sts. Work 3⅛ ins (8 cm) in double rib. Continue for 13⅜ ins (34 cm) in st st, ending on wrong side of work. Now work armhole shaping by binding off 3 sts at beg of next 2 rows and dec 1 st at beg and end of next knit row. Continue straight for 7⅝ ins (20 cm) in st st. Bind off.

Front: cast on 50 sts. Work 3⅛ ins (8 cm) in double rib. Continue for 7⅝ ins (20 cm) in st st. Break off yarn.

Pocket: Using spare needle, on right side of work pick up 50 sts from last row of double rib and work over the st st for 3⅛ ins (8 cm) in double rib. Now decrease 1 st at each end of next 16 rows and then continue straight on these 18 sts in double rib for a further 2 ins (5 cm). Slip 16 sts from main work on to a spare needle and, holding the needle with st st parallel to the needle with ribbed panel, work both sets of sts off together in double rib. Continue as for back, working 16 sts at beg and end of each row in st st and central panel in double rib, then decrease as for back armhole shaping. Continue for 2 ins (5 cm) without shaping, ending on wrong side of work.

Divide for neck opening as follows: bind off 2 center sts and work each side straight, keeping rib and st st continuity, for 5½ ins (14 cm). Bind off all sts worked in st st but keep the ribbed sts on separate needles.

Sleeves: cast on 30 sts. Work for 3⅛ ins (8 cm) in double rib. Continue for 13⅜ ins (34 cm) in st st, increasing 1 st at each end of every 6th row worked on right side of work. Work armhole shaping as for back. Bind off. Make second sleeve.

Finishing: join front and back shoulder seams. Work in double rib on sts left on needle at right side of neck opening, pick up and work in double rib the stitches from neck back and then work in double rib sts left on needle at left side of neck opening. Continue in double rib for 7⅞ ins (20 cm). Sew sides together, and set sleeves into armholes.

Hooded sweater

Materials: 10 skeins (1¾ oz/50 gr) fingering weight yarn in white; small amounts of wine red, light yellow, green, gray, warm brown, red, salmon pink, deep yellow; 1 pr of no 7 needles and 2 spare needles of same size; 1 crochet hook no G/6.

Stitches used: stockinette stitch, double rib (see page 66), garter stitch, corded edging or shrimp stitch (see page 36).

Back: cast on 50 sts. Knit 3⅛ ins (8 cm) in double rib then work 13⅜ ins (34 cm) as follows: *5 rows in st st, purl one row to give a ridge on right side of work*.

Now start shaping raglan shoulders by decreasing 1 stitch, over next 4⅜ ins (11 cm) at each end of alternate rows (on right side of work), keeping continuity of pattern. Break off yarn and leave sts on a spare needle.

Front: work exactly as back until decreases for raglan shoulders are due to start, ending with a wrong side row – 13⅜ ins (34 cm). Now divide front for neck opening by working half the row and binding off the center stitch. Each side is now worked separately, decreasing at shoulder edge as for back. Break off yarn and leave both sets of stitches on a spare needle.

Sleeves: (make 2) cast on 24 sts. Work 3⅛ ins (8 cm) in double rib. Continue in pattern of 5 rows st st, 1 row purl, for 12 ins (30 cm), increasing 1 stitch at each end of every 6th row, on right side of work.

Now decrease for raglan shoulder at both ends of row, as for back. Leave remaining stitches on a spare needle.

Hood: With white yarn, cast on 76 sts. Work in pattern (5 rows st st, 1 row purl) for 5⅛ ins (13 cm). Changing color every 2 rows and working in garter st, continue for 3⅛ ins (8 cm), ending with 2 rows in white. Bind off. Fold in half (wrong side out) and join the 2 edges together on the opposite side to the colored bands. Steam lightly under a damp cloth and turn hood right side out.

Hooded sweater

Finishing: join sides, sew up sleeve seams and set sleeves in position. Pick up all the stitches from the spare needles, in the following order: right front, one sleeve, the back, the second sleeve and finally the left front ending at center opening. Work in garter st on all these stitches in the same color rotation as for hood, changing the color every 2 rows but omitting final 2 rows in white. Bind off.

Stitch hood neatly to neck opening from wrong side – excluding the center front opening, of course. This opening can then be finished off with crocheted corded edging (shrimp stitch) which should continue right round edge of Hood.

Blue pullover

Materials: 12 skeins (1¾ oz/50 gr) blue sport weight; 1 set of 4 double-ended needles no 00; 1 pr of no 1 needles.

Stitches used: single rib (see page 69), stockinette stitch; reversed stockinette stitch (purl side is right side).

Back: with no 1 needles cast on 125 sts, using the tubular method. Work 4 ins (10 cm) in single rib. Continue for 9½ ins (24 cm) in reverse st st, ending with a knit row. Now begin decorative sun-ray pattern: start with p57, k11, p57. Work 1 row exactly as sts appear on needle. Keeping main fabric in reverse st st,

Blue pullover

work center panel as follows:
1st row: *k2, yo, k2 tog, k3, k2 tog, yo, k2*.
2nd and all even rows: p11.
3rd row: *k3, yo, k2 tog, k1, k2 tog, yo, k3*.
5th row: *k4, yo, sl1, k2 tog, psso, yo, k4*.
6th row: p11.
This represents 1 complete motif.
On next row: p32, k11, p13, k11, p13, k11, p32.
Work 5 rows exactly as stitches appear on needle.
Now repeat 1st–6th rows on both side and center panels, keeping main fabric in reverse st st.
Work 2 rows exactly as sts appear on needle.
Next row: (right side of work): p9, k11, p13, k11, p13, k11, p13, k11, p9.
Work 7 rows exactly as sts appear on needle.
Now start raglan shaping by decreasing 3 sts at beg of next 2 rows, at the same time working 1st 2 rows of motif across all panels. Continue in motif, decreasing 1 stitch at each end of every right side row. Still decreasing in the same way for raglan shaping, work motif every 6 rows on all the panels – it is important to remember that the panels to the left of center panel must be moved 1 stitch to the right every 5 rows while the panels on the right must be moved 1 stitch to the left every 5 rows.
Continue until work measures 23⅝ ins (60 cm) from beginning. Bind off.
Front: work exactly as back.
Sleeves: (make 2) cast on 60 sts.
Work 4 ins (10 cm) in single rib.
Change to reverse st st and work 13⅜ ins (34 cm), gradually widening sleeve by increasing 1 st at each end of a purl row until 13⅜ ins (34 cm) in width is reached. At the same time, when work measures 9 ins (23 cm)

and a knit row has been worked, introduce motif as follows: Next row: p38, k11, p38. Work 1 row as sts appear on needle and then 1 motif as for center panel on back.
Next row: (right side of work) p13, k11, p13, k11, p13, k11, p13. Work 7 rows exactly as sts appear on needle.
Next 6 rows: (right side of work) work motif on all 3 panels, keeping main fabric in reverse st st. Work 6 rows exactly as sts appear on needle. When the sleeve is the desired length to the under-arm, work raglan shaping as for back. Continue pattern in this way – moving the left panel 1 stitch to the right every 5 rows and the right panel 1 stitch to the left every 5 rows, at the same time working the motifs every 6 rows – until work measures 24½ ins (62 cm) from beginning.
Finishing: with the double-pointed needles, pick up all the sts evenly on right side of neck opening starting with the back, then across top of left sleeve, across front and finally across top of right sleeve. 1st round: *k2 tog* (this will leave half the no of sts originally picked up).
2nd and all foll rounds: single rib. Continue until neck ribbing measures 3⅛ ins (8 cm). Bind off loosely. Join sides and sleeve seams. Make a flat seam to join raglan shoulders of sleeves to front and back. Fold neck ribbing inwards and stitch in place with small invisible stitches, being careful to retain elasticity of neck opening.

Cap-sleeved pink sweater in double seed stitch

Cap-sleeved pink sweater in double seed stitch

Materials: 6 skeins (1¾ oz/60 gr) sport weight yarn in pink; 1 pr of no 2 needles.

Stitches used: single rib (see page 69), double seed stitch (see page 76).

Back: cast on 116 sts. Work 2⅜ ins (6 cm) in single rib. Continue in double seed st for 9½ ins (24 cm), increasing 1 stitch at each end of row every 3⅛ ins (8 cm). Now increase 1 stitch at each end of next 10 rows. Cast on 15 sts at each end of next row and continue for 6⅝ ins (17 cm). Starting on right side of work, bind off 12 sts at beg of next 4 rows and 13 sts at beg of next 6 rows. Bind off the remaining 46 sts.

Front: work exactly as Back.

Finishing: sew side and shoulder seams.

Brown sweater

Materials: 5 skeins (3½ oz/50 gr) worsted weight yarn in brown; 1 pr of no 10½ needles: 1 crochet hook size K/10¼; 1 set of no 10½ double-pointed needles.

Stitches used: garter stitch, stockinette stitch, single rib (see page 69).

Back: cast on 42 sts. Work 1½ ins (4 cm) in garter stitch, then continue for another 1/¾ ins (45 cm) in st st. Bind off.

Front: cast on 42 sts. Work 1½ ins (4 cm) in garter st and then 2¾ ins (7 cm) in st st. Mark row, continue in st st for a further 6 ins (15 cm) ending with a wrong side row. Leave sts on a spare needle. With the aid of the crochet hook, pick up the centre 24 sts of marked row and knit as follows, with right side facing: 1st row: knit; 2nd row: k3, p18, k3. Rep these 2 rows (keeping 3 sts in garter st at each side and center panel in st st) for 6 ins (15 cm). Leave sts on a spare needle.

Return to main fabric and, with right side facing, k9; now with the aid of the crochet hook, knit each of the next 24 sts with the corresponding stitch of pocket; end the row with k9. (These sts will all be worked in st st from the next row on.) Continue in

Brown sweater

st st until work measures 17 ins (42 cm) from beg. For neck opening, work on each side separately. In st st, work a round neckline (see page 43). Bring work to same length as Back and bind off. Work other side of neck opening to match.

Sleeves: (make 2) cast on 34 sts. Work 3½ ins (9 cm) in garter st and continue for 15¾ ins (40 cm) in st st. Bind off.

Finishing: join side and shoulder seams. With the 4 needles, pick up 68 sts evenly round neck opening and work 9⅞ ins (25 cm) in rounds of single rib. Bind off loosely. Join sleeve seams and set sleeves into armholes; fold cuffs back at wrists.

Plaid/striped sweater

Materials: 6 skeins (1¾ oz/50 gr) each of pink, blue and light green mohair; 1 pr of no 5 needles; 1 crochet hook size F/5; 3 silk cords about 3 yds long in pink, blue and green.

Stitches used: reversed stockinette stitch, single rib (see page 69), single crochet, corded edge (see page 36).

Back: cast on 72 sts by tubular method. In single rib, work 1 row in blue, 1 row in green and 1 row in pink. From now on, the back and front are worked with 2 strands at a time, sometimes in contrasting colors and sometimes in same color. Working with pink and green yarn, knit 12 sts in reverse st st, remembering to weave the blue through the wrong side of work (this is done by carrying it over, at back of work, on alternate sts keeping tension flexible). Now drop green and join the blue in with the pink (each

time a color is changed, cross the strands of yarn, at front of work) and work 12 sts. Drop blue and join in another pink strand from a new ball; work 12 sts. Now drop one pink strand, join in green from a new ball and work another 12 sts. Drop the green and join blue from a new ball and work 12 sts. Drop blue and join in another pink to work the last 12 sts. There should now be 7 separate balls of yarn being worked, of which only one (for this line of squares, one of the pink balls) is used all the time.

Continue in the same way for 14 rows.

Now change the basic color (i.e. the one which is used all the time) to blue for the 2nd line of squares, green for the 3rd line, pink for the 4th and so on until 9 lines of squares have been worked and work measures 20⅞ ins (53 cm) and the colors have been blended as shown in diagram.

Front: work exactly as back. The two sides are identical.

Sleeves: (make 2) cast on 60 sts by tubular method. In single rib, work 1 row blue, 1 row green, 1 row pink and then continue for 21¼ ins (54 cm) in reverse st st, increasing at regular intervals at each end of a right side row until there are 80 sts on needle, with the following color pattern: 4 rows pink, 2 rows blue, 2 rows green. Now bind off 34 sts at beg of next 2 rows and work in reverse st st on rem center 12 sts in double pink yarn, for 2¾ ins (7 cm) (width of one square on main fabric) and then in 1 thread each of pink and blue for another 2¾ ins (7 cm). Bind off.

Finishing: join side and sleeve seams. Sew shoulders, formed by sleeve extensions, to front and back with a flat seam and set sleeves into armholes with a flat seam. With pink yarn, work 1 round of single crochet

Plaid/striped sweater

and 1 round of corded edge round the neckline. Plait the 3 cords together and cut 3 lengths for waist and wrists. Thread through lower edges of sweater and sleeves.

Diagram for plaid/striped sweater

Brown and beige sweater

Materials: worsted weight yarn, 3½ oz/100 gr skeins, 2 brown; 4 beige; 1 pr of no 5 needles; 1 pr of no 6 needles; 1 set of double-pointed needles no 5.

Stitches used: fancy stitch no 1 (see page 104); double rib (see page 66).

Back: With brown yarn and no 5 needles, cast on 100 sts.

Work 3⅛ ins (8 cm) in double rib. Changing to beige yarn and no 6 needles, work straight for 11 ins (28 cm) in fancy stitch no 1.

For armhole shaping, decrease 1 stitch after the 1st st and on the next to last st of every other row (right side of work only), until 62 sts remain. Leave sts on a spare needle.

Front: work exactly as back.

Sleeves: (make 2). With brown yarn cast on 50 sts, work 4 ins (10 cm) in double rib. Changing to beige yarn and no 6 needles, work 13 ins (33 cm) in fancy st no 1, increasing 1 stitch at each side eleven times, at evenly spaced intervals (72 sts).

Now shape for raglan shoulders by decreasing 1 st at each end of every other row (right side of work only), as for back, until 31 sts remain. Leave sts on a spare needle.

Collar: with brown yarn and set of no 5 needles, with front of work facing, divide the sts from front, 1 sleeve, back, 1 sleeve equally between the 3 working needles (62 sts on each). Work as follows:

1st–10th rows: *p4, k2* (186 sts).
11th–20th rows: *p3, k2* (dec 4 p sts to 3: 155 sts).

Brown and beige sweater

Tweed sweater with white insertions

21st row: *p2, k2* (dec 3 p sts to 2: 124 sts).
Continue in rounds of double rib for a further 8¼ ins (21 cm).
Bind off very loosely.
Finishing: sew raglan shoulder seams with a flat seam. Join side and sleeve seams.

Tweed sweater with white insertions

Materials: 6 skeins (3½ oz/100 gr) tweed-mixture worsted weight yarn and 2 in white; 1 pr of no 9 needles; 1 set of double-pointed needles no 9.
Stitches used: stockinette stitch, single rib (see page 69), English rib (see page 66).
Back: cast on 68 sts by tubular method and work 3 rows in the same method. Continue for 3⅛ ins (8 cm) in stockinette stitch and then work 20⅞ ins (53 cm) in English rib. Bind off.
Front: cast on 68 sts by tubular method and work 3 rows in the same method. Continue for 3⅛ ins (8 cm) in st st and then work 11 ins (28 cm) in English rib. Now start decreasing for V-neck (see p44), working on each side separately. When work measures the same as back, bind off.
Sleeves: (make 2) cast on 40 sts by tubular method and work 3 rows in same method. Continue for 2 ins (5 cm) in st st and then work 14½ ins (37 cm) in English rib, increasing 1 st at each end of row 6 times on right side of work at evenly spaced intervals. Join in white yarn and work a further 2 ins (5 cm) in st st increasing 1 st at each end of row 3 times. Keep sts on needle and sew directly on to front and back, using duplicate stitch (see p58).

White and cerise sweater

Finishing: sew all shoulder, side and sleeve seams.

With right side of work facing and using the set of double-pointed needles, with white yarn pick up evenly the stitches around neck opening and work the V-neck (see page 44) in single rib, ¾ in (2 cm) in white, then ¾ in (2 cm) in mixture. Now work 2 rounds in tubular st and bind off by the same method.

White and cerise sweater

Materials: 5 skeins (3½ oz/100 gr) worsted weight yarn in white and 1 in cerise; 1 pr of no 10½ needles.
Stitches used: garter stitch, stockinette stitch.
Back: with white yarn, cast on 50 sts. Work 2¾ ins (7 cm) in garter stitch and then continue in st st, introducing the cerise yarn and working the lower border from diagram no 2 on p131 for 2 ins (5 cm). Now work 2⅜ ins (6 cm) with white yarn in st st and then, introducing cerise yarn again, follow diagram no 1 on p131. After a further 2⅜ ins (6 cm) in white yarn, rep diagram no 2. Continue to work straight with white yarn for another 6 ins (15 cm) in st st and then for a further 6¼ ins (16 cm) in garter st. Bind off.
Front: work exactly as back.
Sleeves: (make 2) With white yarn, cast on 32 sts. Work 2¾ ins (7 cm) in garter st and then, alternating white and cerise yarns, continue in st st, working diagram no 2 for 2 ins (5 cm). Now work 2⅜ ins (6 cm) in white yarn and then follow diagram no 1, in two colors, for 2⅜ ins (6 cm). Work a further 2⅜ ins (6 cm) in white yarn and then rep diagram no 2 for another 2 ins (5 cm). With white yarn, continue for 7 ins (18 cm) in st st. Bind off.
Finishing: join front and back side seams for 17¾ ins (45 cm) from lower edge; join shoulder seams, leaving 10¼ ins (26 cm) unstitched at center for neck opening. Join sleeve seams and sew sleeves into armholes with duplicate st (see page 58).

Red sleeveless slipover

Materials: 3 skeins (1¾ oz/50 gr) fingering weight yarn in red; 1 pr no 5 needles.

Stitches used: single rib (see page 69), stockinette stitch, garter stitch.
Back: cast on 48 sts. Work 2⅜ ins (6 cm) in single rib and then 11⅞ ins (30 cm) in st st. For next 1⅛ ins (3 cm) work first and last 10 sts of each row in garter st, continuing in st st over rest of row. Bind off 5 sts at beg of next 2 rows for armhole shaping and continue straight for 7⅞ ins (20 cm), retaining 5 sts in garter st at each end of every row. Bind off.
Front: work as for back until armhole shaping. Bind off center 18 sts and work each side separately until same length as back.

Red sleeveless slipover

Finishing: join side and shoulder seams. Pick up the 18 sts bound off at center front and work a strip in garter st the same length as entire neck opening; it should overlap in the front where it rejoins picked-up sts. Bind off. Sew neatly into place.

Bolero in mock marabou

Materials: 3 skeins (3½ oz/100 gr) of marabou yarn in blue; 1¾ oz/50 gr worsted weight yarn in blue; 1 pr of no 10½ needles and 1 spare needle.
Stitches used: garter stitch; stockinette stitch.
This bolero is made in one piece.
Cast on sts to a width of 39½ ins (100 cm) and work in st st for 9⅞ ins (25 cm), ending with a wrong side row. With a contrasting thread, mark 2 points 9 ins (23 cm) from each edge; k to within 4 sts of first marker and bind off 8 sts (4 bound-off sts will be the start of front armhole shaping and 4 will be the start of back armhole shaping); k to within 4 sts of second marker, bind off 8 sts and work to end of row. The fabric is now divided into 3, 2 fronts and back. Transfer sts of 1 front and back to spare needle. Work on rem front, decreasing 1 st at armhole edge on every right side row, until work measures 3½ ins (9 cm) wide. Bind off. Work back in a similar way, decreasing 1 st at each armhole edge on every right side row, until work measures 13¾ ins (35 cm) wide. Bind off.
Work 2nd front as 1st front. Bind off.
Finishing: join shoulder seams. With blue yarn, pick up evenly all sts on lower edge and work 4 rows in garter st. Bind off loosely.
Cast on 5 sts in blue worsted weight yarn and work in garter st until strip measures the same as both front edges and back of neck. Sew this

Bolero in mock marabou

Striped skirt in mohair

strip neatly into place.
For pockets, with marabou yarn cast on sts to a width of 4¾ ins (12 cm) and work 2¾ ins (7 cm) in garter st and then change to blue yarn and work a further ¾ ins (2 cm). Bind off. Mark positions for a pocket near lower edge of each front and stitch neatly into place from right side, as for patch-pockets.

Striped skirt in mohair

Materials: 1 skein (1¾ oz/50 gr) mohair yarn in each color: gray, cream black, mauve; 1 pr of no 5 needles; elastic to fit waist comfortably; 2 hooks; 1 4 in (10 cm) zipper.
Stitches used: stockinette stitch and reversed stockinette st. The skirt consists of 3 equal panels. For each

panel, cast on 75 sts in gray mohair, and work 6⅝ ins (17 cm) in reverse st st. Change color now, and every 6⅝ ins (17 cm); bind off when four bands have been completed. Make 2 more identical panels.

Finishing: join the 3 panels together, taking care to join bands so that there is no break in the line. One of the seams will come at center back; leave 4 ins (10 cm) of this unstitched at waist edge.

With mauve mohair, pick up every other st around waist, slightly gathering it. Work 4 ins (10 cm) in st st and bind off. Fold this waistband inwards and stitch neatly to inside top of skirt, still retaining back opening. Before sewing up ends of waistband, insert elastic and stitch in place at each end, at the same time closing ends of waistband. Now insert zipper, using very small stitches, and sew on the 2 hooks inside top of opening. Finish off back opening by turning edges in and sewing neatly to form narrow hems.

Poncho

Materials: 9 skeins (3½ oz/100 gr) worsted weight yarn in dark blue and 1 in white, rust, bright blue and gray; 1 pr of no 11 needles; crochet hook size K/10¼.

Stitches used: stockinette stitch, single crochet, corded edge (see page 36).

The poncho is started at the back and worked in one piece. With dark blue yarn, cast on 48 sts and work 4¾ ins (12 cm) in st st. Continue in st st for 15 ins (38 cm), increasing 1 st at each side on every row until there are 86 sts on the needle. The work will now measure 19¾ ins (50 cm) from start.

Working straight, introduce bands of color as follows: 4 rows bright blue,

2 rows dark blue, 2 rows bright blue, 4 rows dark blue, 10 rows rust (on 8th rust row, divide work in half by working 2 sts tog twice at center (42nd and 43rd, 44th and 45th) and continue to work on each half by using 2 balls of yarn in each color). When 10th rust row has been worked continue with 4 rows gray, 4 rows bright blue, 6 rows dark blue, 4 rows bright blue, 4 rows gray, 10 rows rust, 4 rows dark blue, 2 rows bright blue, 2 rows dark blue, 4 rows bright blue, 2 rows white. Still working with white yarn, on next row, cast on 4 sts at neck opening, working whole length of row on one ball of yarn.

Now begin jacquard design by following diagram no 7 (see page 132) on center 46 sts.

Continue for a further 11 ins (28 cm) in dark blue and then, decreasing 1 st at each side on every row, work another 4¾ ins (12 cm). Bind off remaining 48 sts.

Finishing: with dark blue yarn, work 4 rounds of sc along entire outer edge of poncho. With dark blue yarn, work a corded edge all round neck opening. On lower front edge work, in sc, 1 row dark blue, 1 row bright blue, 1 row dark blue, 1 row rust; on lower back edge work 1 row sc in bright blue. Finish off both lower edges and side openings (i.e. entire outer edge) in dark blue yarn with a corded edge.

Evening jacket in mock marabou with choker neckband

Jacket. Materials: 10 skeins (3½ oz/100 gr) marabou yarn in black; 1 pr of no 11 needles; 1 31½ in (80 cm) separating zipper.
Stitches used: garter stitch, stockinette stitch.
Back: cast on sts to a width of 24 ins (60 cm). Work 2 ins (5 cm) in garter st and then a further 17¾ ins (45 cm) in st st.
Now shape armholes by binding off sts to reduce width by 2 ins (5 cm) on each side so that fabric now measures 19¾ ins (50 cm) wide. Continue for a further 6 ins (15 cm) in st st. Bind off.
Half front: cast on sts to a width of 12 ins (30 cm). Work 2 ins (5 cm) in garter st and then 8 ins (20 cm) in st st. Now work a vertical pocket (see p43) 5 ins (13 cm) from lower to upper edge and positioned just over an inch (3 cm) in from side edge. Continue for another 4¾ ins (12 cm) in st st.
Now shape armhole by binding off sts to reduce width of work by 2¾ ins (7 cm). Continue for a further 6 ins (15 cm) in st st. Bind off.
Work a second half front to match, working pocket and armhole shaping on opposite side.
Sleeves: (make 2) cast on sts to a width of 15¾ ins (40 cm). Work 2 ins (5 cm) in garter st and then 20½ ins (52 cm) in st st.
Hood: cast on sts to a width of 19¾ ins (50 cm). Work 35½ ins (90 cm) in st st. Bind off. Fold in half lengthwise and sew the two long edges together.
Finishing: join side and shoulder seams; sew sleeve seams and set sleeves into armholes. Stitch hood to neckline and sew zipper to both center fronts and up nearly 8 ins (20 cm) of each side of hood.

Choker neckband. Materials: ½ skein marabou yarn in black; 1 pr of no 11 needles.
Stitch used: garter stitch.
Cast on sts to a width of 8 ins (20 cm). Work 24 ins (60 cm) in garter st. Bind off. Fold the strip in half lengthwise and sew the two ends together.

Turquoise and silver evening 2-piece and purse

Materials: 16 skeins (1¾ oz/50 gr) turquoise and silver mixture yarn; 1 pr of no 2 needles; 1 set of no 2 double-pointed needles; length of elastic to fit waist comfortably.
Stitches used: reversed stockinette stitch, single rib (see page 69). This evening 2-piece consists of a long skirt and top worked in the same material and stitches.
Skirt. Back: cast on 200 sts. Work 35½ ins (90 cm) in reverse st st gradually decreasing 25 sts at each side until 150 sts remain on the needle. Continue for a further 8⅝ ins (22 cm) in single rib.
Front: work exactly as back.
Finishing: join side seams. Turn in 1½ ins (4 cm) of lower edge and sew into place with small, neat stitches to form a hem. Turn in 1⅛ ins (3 cm) of upper edge and sew into place to form waistband; thread elastic through waistband and stitch ends together firmly.
Top. Back: cast on 60 sts and work 2¾ ins (7 cm) in single rib. Continue for 9½ ins (24 cm) in reverse st st.
Now begin decreasing for raglan shaping and, at the same time, for

Evening jacket in mock marabou with choker neckband

Turquoise and silver evening 2-piece and purse

neck edge as follows: divide work in half, leaving 30 sts on a spare needle; at armhole edge, decrease 1 st every 4 rows on right side of work and 1 st every 2 rows at neck edge on right side of work until no stitches remain. Return to sts on spare needle and work opposite side to match.

Front: work exactly as back.
Sleeves: (work 2) cast on 60 sts and work 3⅛ ins (8 cm) in single rib. Continue in reverse st st, gradually increasing 12 sts at each side until there are 84 sts on needle, for 13 ins (33 cm). Now decrease 1 stitch at each end of every 4th row on right

side of work until 50 sts remain. Bind off. These stitches will form part of the basis for neckline ribbing.

Finishing: join side and sleeve seams. Sew front and back to raglan sleeves with a flat seam. Using the set of needles pick up all the stitches evenly round neck opening (formed by the front, sleeve, back and sleeve) and work 2 ins (5 cm) in single rib.

Purse. Materials: 1 skein (1¾ oz/50 gr) wool and Lurex mixture; 1 pr of no 2 needles; 1 crochet hook size E/4.

Stitches used: stockinette stitch, single crochet, corded edge (see page 36).

Cast on 4 sts and work 2 rows in st st. Now start increasing 1 st at each end of every right side row until there are 40 sts on needle.

Work straight in st st, for 9½ ins (24 cm). Bind off.

To make up and complete: fold the straight piece of fabric in half (rather like an envelope) and join sides with a row of sc. Using yarn double, finish off edge of flap by working 1 row of sc and then the corded edge. Attach a fastener.

Patterns for men

This chapter consists of a few basic patterns – a jacket, sweaters for country or sports wear, vests, etc. But the variations that can be made on these themes are endless and many useful and attractive garments may be produced with a little inventiveness.

Olive green jacket

Materials: 8 skeins (3½ oz/100 gr) worsted weight yarn in olive green; 1 pr of no 10½ needles.

Stitches used: twisted rib (see page 69), Gaston's stitch (see page 75).

Back: cast on 68 sts by the tubular method and continue for 3½ ins (9 cm) in twisted rib. Now change to Gaston's st and work straight until back measures 18 ins (46 cm). For armhole shaping, bind off 2 sts at beg of next 4 rows and then dec 1 st at each end of next 2 rows.

Continue straight until back measures 26 ins (66 cm) from start. Bind off 7 sts at beg of next 6 rows and then bind off rem sts for back of neck.

Right front: cast on 48 sts by the tubular method and work 3½ ins (9 cm) in twisted rib. Keeping 10 sts at center front edge in twisted rib and working rem 38 sts in Gaston's st, continue straight until piece measures 18 ins (46 cm).

For armhole shaping bind off 2 sts twice and dec 1 st twice at armhole edge.

Continue straight until right front measures 23⅝ ins (60 cm) from start. For neck shaping, bind off the 10 border sts and then dec 1 st on every row at neck edge until only 21 shoulder sts remain. Bind off shoulder sts, starting from outer edge, in 3 groups of 7. Break yarn and fasten off.

Left front: work as for right front, making 7 buttonholes (see page 40) at evenly spaced intervals in the twisted rib border.

Sleeves: (make 2) cast on 36 sts by

the tubular method and work 4⅜ ins (11 cm) in twisted rib. Continue for 17 ins (43 cm) in Gaston's st, increasing 1 st at each end of row 9 times at regular intervals. (Sleeve now measures 21¼ ins (54 cm) from start.

To shape top, bind off 4 sts at beg of next 2 rows and then dec 1 st on each row until 14 sts remain. Bind off.

Finishing: join side and shoulder seams. Sew sleeve seams together and set sleeves into armholes. Starting from center left front and continuing across back to center right front, pick up 66 sts evenly and work in twisted rib for 6 ins (15 cm). Bind off fairly loosely.

White pullover

Materials: 9 skeins (3½ oz/100 gr) worsted weight yarn in white; 1 pr of no 11 needles, 1 cable needle, 1

Olive green jacket

White pullover

spare needle.

Stitches used: stockinette stitch and reversed stockinette st, single rib (see page 69), single cable stitch (see page 92), double seed stitch (see page 76), garter stitch.

Back: cast on 54 sts and work 2 ins (5 cm) in single rib. Now continue in various patterns as follows: first 8 sts in r st st, 1 st st, 3 r st st, 6 single cable (cable 3 sts over 3 sts), 3 r st st, 1 st st, 10 dbl seed st, 1 st st, 3 r st st, 6 single cable, 3 r st st, 1 st st, 8 r st st. Continue in this way for 13¾ ins (35 cm).

For raglan shaping, dec 1 st at each side of every right side row, working

first and last 2 sts in st st. Continue decreasing for 8⅝ ins (22 cm); bind off remaining stitches.

Front: work as for back as far as start of raglan shaping, ending with a wrong side row. Next row: 2 sts in st st, dec 1, work 18 sts in pattern and leave these 21 sts on a spare needle. Bind off next 10 sts and work in pattern to last 4 sts. Dec 1 stitch and work 2 st st. Continue, decreasing at right side at raglan edge exactly as for back.

Return to sts left on spare needle and complete left side in the same way, reversing shapings.

Sleeves: (make 2) cast on 26 sts and

work 2⅜ ins (6 cm) in single rib. Work in pattern for 13 ins (33 cm) increasing 1 st at each end of every 6th row until there are 12 sts in r st st at both ends of row. Start pattern as follows:

6 r st st, 1 st st, 3 r st st, 6 single cable, 3 r st st, 1 st st, 6 r st st.

When work measures 15⅜ ins (39 cm), start decreasing for raglan shaping, working first and last 2 sts of each row in st st.

Finishing: join side and sleeve seams. Sew sleeves to front and back pieces with flat seams. For neck border, cast on 5 sts and make a straight strip in garter st long enough to fit neatly all the way around neck opening. Bind off. Stitch this strip into place with a flat seam, with cast on and bound off stitches meeting the 10 sts bound off at center front.

White and gray sweater

Materials: 5 skeins (3½ oz/100 gr) worsted weight yarn in white and 3 in gray tweed; 1 pr of no 11 needles; 1 crochet hook size K/10¼; 1 spare needle.

Stitches used: single rib (see p69); stockinette stitch; garter stitch.

Back: with white yarn, cast on 42 sts. Work 2¾ ins (7 cm) in single rib and 5½ ins (14 cm) in st st. Now change to gray tweed yarn and work 3⅛ ins (8 cm); in white work 4 ins (10 cm); in gray work another 3⅛ ins (8 cm) in white work a further 4 ins (10 cm), finishing with 3⅛ ins (8 cm) in gray. Bind off.

Front: with white, cast on 42 sts. Work 2¾ ins (7 cm) in single rib and 5½ ins (14 cm) in st st. Now change to gray and work 3⅛ ins (8 cm) and then 2⅜ ins (6 cm) in white, ending with a wrong side row. Transfer these sts to a spare needle (or introduce another needle of same size) to work on pocket.

With crochet hook and using white, pick up 22 sts from center of first st st band in white, about 3⅛ ins (8 cm) from beg of st st. Work as follows: 3 sts garter st, 12 st st, 3 garter st. Continue in this way for 2⅜ ins (6 cm); change to gray and work 3⅛ ins (8 cm) and then another 2⅜ ins (6 cm) in white.

Return to main fabric and work 10 sts in st st; now knit each pocket stitch with corresponding stitch in main fabric, using crochet hook to ease sts off back needle; knit to end of row. Continue, with white yarn, in st st for a further 1½ ins (4 cm). Now divide for V-neck by transferring half the sts (21) to a spare needle and, keeping stripes as for back, dec 1 stitch at neck edge on alternate rows for 20 rows; work a further 4 ins (10 cm) straight. Bind off.

Sleeves: (make 2) with white, cast on 28 sts. Work 2⅜ ins (6 cm) in single rib. Continue in st st, working stripes as explained below, increasing 1 stitch at each end of row at regular intervals, until there are 42 sts on needle. Stripes are worked as follows: white 4⅜ ins (11 cm); gray 3⅛ ins (8 cm); white 4 ins (10 cm); gray 1½ ins (4 cm); white 4 ins (10 cm). Bind off.

Finishing: join side seams, leaving 8⅝ ins (22 cm) open at top for armhole; join shoulder seams; sew up sleeve seams and set sleeves into armholes. For V-neck ribbing and collar, cast on 58 sts and work 1½ ins (4 cm) in single rib. Bind off the first 17 sts, rib next 24 sts and slip remaining 17 sts onto a spare needle. Work in single rib on central 24 sts for a further 4¾ ins (12 cm). Bind off. Rejoin yarn to stitches kept aside on spare needle and bind off. Sew ribbing and collar neatly into

White and gray sweater

place with a flat seam, forming the point at V by slightly overlapping the two ends of ribbing.

Gray sweater

Materials: 10 skeins (1¾ oz/50 gr) sport weight yarn in gray; 1 pr of no 4 needles; 1 set of double-pointed no 4 needles; 1 cable needle.

Stitches used: single rib (see page 69), stockinette stitch and reversed stockinette st, 3-stitch cable (see page 92).

Back: cast on 120 sts and work 2¾

Gray sweater

ins (7 cm) in single rib. Change to st st and work straight for 13 ins (33 cm). For armhole shaping, bind off 3 sts at beg of next 2 rows, bind off 2 sts at beg of next 2 rows and then dec 1 st at each end of next 3 right side rows (104 sts remain). Continue without shaping for a further 6 ins (15 cm). Now shape shoulders by binding off 11 sts at beg of next 6 rows (33 sts decreased each side). Bind off remaining 38 sts at center back.

Front: cast on 120 sts and work 2¾ ins (7 cm) in single rib. Now create panels by working next row as follows: 20 sts in st st, 4 r st st, 12 sts in 3-stitch cable 4 r st st, 40 st st, 4 r st st, 12sts in 3-stitch cable, 4 r st st, 20 st st.

Continue in this way for 13 ins (33 cm) then decrease for armhole shaping as for back (this will reduce st st panels at each end of row to 12 sts). When work measures 22⅞ ins (58 cm) from start, bind off center 22 sts and work on each side separately, decreasing 1 stitch at neck edge until work measures same as back at beginning of shoulder shaping. Still decreasing at neck edge, bind off 11 sts at shoulder edge on alternate rows 3 times. Bind off rem sts.

Sleeves: (make 2) cast on 64 sts and work 2¾ ins (7 cm) in single rib. Change to st st and work 15¾ ins (40 cm), increasing 1 stitch at each end of the row, at regular intervals, until there are 80 sts on needle. Now work armhole shaping, as for

Blue sweater

back, but continue to decrease 1 stitch at each end of right side rows until sleeve measures 22 ins (56 cm) from start. Bind off.

Finishing: join side and shoulder seams. Sew up sleeve seams and set sleeves into armholes. With the set of double-pointed needles, pick up all the stitches evenly around neck opening, divide them equally between 3 of the needles, and work in single rib for 7 ins (18 cm). Bind off loosely.

Blue sweater

Materials: 8 skeins (3½ oz/100 gr) worsted weight yarn in blue; 1 pr of no 9 needles.

Stitches used: single rib (see page 69), Sylvia's rib stitch (see page 70).

Back: cast on 54 sts and work 1½ ins (4 cm) in single rib. Now change to Sylvia's rib st and work 15 ins (38 cm), ending with a wrong side row. Work should now measure 16½ ins (42 cm) from start. Shape for armholes by decreasing 3 sts at each end of row, 2 sts at each end of next right side row and then decreasing 1 st at each end of next right side row. Continue without shaping for a further 7⅞ ins (20 cm). Bind off.

Front: work as for back but, when working armhole shaping, divide stitches at center front and decrease for V-neck at the same time (see page 44). Work each side separately for 7⅞ ins (20 cm). Bind off.

Sleeves: (make 2) cast on 26 sts and

Brown vest

work 2⅜ ins (6 cm) in single rib. Continue in Sylvia's rib st, increasing 1 stitch at each end of every 8th row (right side of work) until work measures 19¾ ins (50 cm). For armhole shaping, decrease as for back and continue decreasing 1 st at each end of every right side row until armhole measures same as back. Bind off. Finishing: join side and shoulder seams; sew up sleeves seams and set sleeves into armholes. Pick up sts round neck and work ¾ in (2 cm) in single rib.

Brown vest

Materials: 7 skeins (1¾ oz/50 gr) sport weight yarn in brown; 1 pr of no 6 needles; 1 set of no 6 dp needles (optional), 4 buttons.

Stitches used: stockinette stitch, double rib (see page 66).

Back: cast on 80 sts and work 2⅜ ins (6 cm) in double rib. Continue straight for 15 ins (38 cm) in st st. Now shape for armholes by decreasing, on right side of work only, as follows: 3 sts at each end of row once, 2 sts at each end of row once, 1 stitch at each end of row once. Continue in st st, without shaping, for 8⅝ ins (22 cm). Bind off center 26 sts and, continuing on each side separately, work 2 rows. Bind off.

Front half: cast on 40 sts and work 2⅜ ins (6 cm) in double rib. Continue straight for 15 ins (38 cm) in st st. Now shape for armhole, as for back, at the same time begin shaping for center front by decreasing 1 stitch every 3 rows until front half measures the same as back.

Work second half to match, reversing shaping.

Finishing: join side and shoulder seams. Pick up all sts evenly (in a number divisible by 4) around each armhole, ensuring that the same number of sts is picked up on both armholes, and work 5 rows in double rib. If a set of needles is used, work in rounds. If 2 needles have been used, sew short edges together with a flat seam. Pick up all the stitches (in a number divisible by 4) along edge of center right front (starting at lower corner), back of neck and down edge of center left front, working 1½ ins (4 cm) in double rib. While working left center front edging, make 4 vertical buttonholes (see page 40) 4 ins (10 cm) apart. Sew on buttons.

Red sleeveless slipover

Materials: 4 skeins (3½ oz/100 gr) bulky weight yarn in red; 1 pr of no 9 needles; 1 set of double-pointed no 9 needles (optional).

Stitches used: stockinette stitch, single rib (see page 69).

Back: cast on 50 sts and work 3 rows in single rib. Continue for 15¾ ins (40 cm) in st st. Now shape for armholes by binding off 5 sts at beg of next 2 rows. Continue in st st for another 9⅞ ins (25 cm). Bind off all sts.

Front: work as for back until 2 ins (5 cm) after armhole shaping has been worked. Bind off center 10 sts and, working each side separately, decrease 1 stitch 5 times at neck edge on every right side row. Continue in st st on remaining 10 sts until work measures same as back.

Finishing: join side and shoulder seams. With set of needles (if preferred), pick up stitches evenly around neck opening and work 4 rounds (or rows) in single rib. Cast off loosely. Work similarly around both armholes, ensuring that the same number of stitches is picked up for each. If 2 needles have been used, sew short edges together with a flat seam.

Red sleeveless slipover

Patterns for children

Knitting for children gives just as much scope to the imagination as knitting for adults. It has one great advantage, too – the little garments, being so much smaller than those for grown-ups, can be made very quickly and, if a little extra wool is bought, every time you decide to make something for a baby or small child, the garment can be unravelled and made larger or even merely lengthened as the child grows.

Cream coat

Materials: 4 skeins (3½ oz/100 gr) worsted weight yarn in white, 1 pr of no 9 needles; 3 spare needles in same size; 2 buttons.
Stitches used: garter stitch, double rib (see page 66).
Back: cast on 42 sts and work 12 ins (30 cm) in garter st. Leave sts on spare needle.
Half front: (make 2) cast on 21 sts and work 12 ins (30 cm) in garter st. Leave sts on spare needle.
Sleeves: (make 2) cast on 22 sts and work 2¾ ins (7 cm) in dbl rib. Continue for 8⅝ ins (22 cm) in garter st. Leave sts on spare needle (with sts left for back and half front).
Now work all sts onto one needle, starting with a half front, then a sleeve, back, sleeve and 2nd half front, as follows: 5 sts in garter st (this will form right center front

Pram coat

178

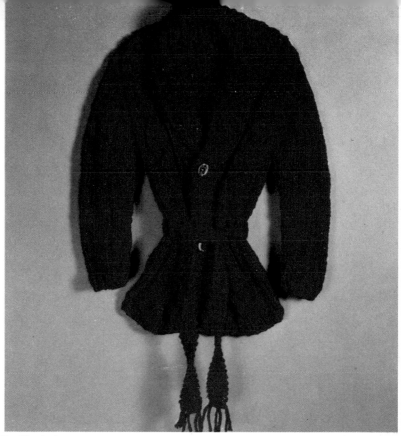

Red jacket

border), *k2, p3*, 5 sts in garter st (for left center front border). While working yoke, make one horizontal buttonhole (see page 40) a few rows from start of garter st border, on left or right side, and a second buttonhole in garter st neckband on same side. To shape the yoke, decrease the p3 by 1 st all the way round thus leaving 2 center front borders in garter st and all sts between in double rib. Continue for 7 ins (18 cm), decreasing one or two more stitches, then work 4 ridges in garter st for neckband.

Finishing: join side seams and sew on buttons.

Red jacket

Materials: 5 skeins (3½ oz/100 gr) worsted weight yarn in red; 1 pr of no 9 needles; 1 cable needle; 1 fairly thick crochet hook; 3 wooden buttons.

Stitches used: stockinette stitch and reversed stockinette st, single rib (see page 69), garter stitch, single cable stitch (see page 92), Sylvia's rib stitch (see page 70), crocheted chain stitch.

Back: cast on 34 sts and work 1½ ins (4 cm) in single rib. Change to Sylvia's rib st and work 11 ins (28 cm). For raglan shaping, work as explained on page 45 for 6 ins (15 cm), keeping the 2 end sts of each row in st st. Bind off all remaining stitches.

Right front: cast on 25 sts and work first row as follows: 18 sts in single rib, 1 st in st st, 5 sts in garter st, 1 st in st st. Continue this pattern, for 1½ ins (4 cm), making a horizontal buttonhole (see page 40) on the 2nd row of the garter st edge. Two more horizontal buttonholes should be made at intervals of 4⅜ ins (11 cm).

Continue in foll pattern: 6 sts in r st st, 6 sts in single cable (cable 3 sts over 3), 6 sts in r st st, 1 st in st st, 5 sts in garter st, 1 st in st st for 11 ins (28 cm).

Now shape for armhole, on right side of work, as for back, at the same time increasing 1 stitch at center front on next 16 rows, working all new stitches in garter st but keeping the last stitch on center front edge in st st. Continue for a further 20 rows without increasing. Bind off.

Left front: work as for right front, reversing shapings and omitting buttonholes.

Sleeves: (make 2) cast on 22 sts and work 1½ ins (4 cm) in single rib. Change to Sylvia's rib st and work 9⅞ ins (25 cm), increasing one stitch at each end of every 7th row. Now decrease for raglan as for back. Bind off.

Finishing: join side seams. Sew up sleeve seams and join sleeves to front and back. Join cast off ends of collar neatly to back neck edge. Sew on buttons. Using crochet hook, make two 1¼ ins (3 cm) lengths of crocheted chain (see page 36) and stitch in place on side seams at waist level to carry belt. Make belt by casting on 5 sts and working 40 ins (100 cm) in garter st. Bind off. Work a little fringing (see page 55) at each end and thread belt through loops. Trim fringing to the required length.

White jacket

Materials. 4 skeins (3½ oz/100 gr) worsted weight yarn in white; 1 pr of no 7 needles; 4 buttons.

Stitches used: single rib (see page 69), stockinette stitch, garter stitch.

Back: cast on 35 sts and work 2¾ ins (7 cm) in single rib. Change to garter st and work 7 ins (18 cm). Now shape armholes by binding off 3 sts at beg of next 2 rows and, at the same time, work the following pattern: *4 sts in garter st, 1 st in st st* 4 sts in garter st. Keeping the continuity of this pattern, work a further 4 ins (10 cm). Bind off.

Half front: (4 vertical buttonholes (see page 40) to be worked at regular intervals on left or right center front border), cast on 21 sts and work 2¾ ins (7 cm) in the following pattern: 1 st in st st, 4 sts in garter st, 16 sts in single rib. Now, keeping 1 st in st st, 4 sts in garter st, 1 st in st st, work rest of row in garter st. Rep this row for 7 ins (18 cm), ending at armhole edge. Bind off 3 sts for armhole shaping and then work 2 ins (5 cm) as follows (retaining center front border as described above): 4 sts in garter st, 1 st in st st, 4 sts in garter st, 1 st in st st, 2 sts in garter st. Finish at center front edge. Bind off 5 sts of border and, keeping continuity of pattern, continue for a further 10 rows, decreasing 1 stitch at beg of every neck edge row (5 decreases). Bind off remaining stitches.

Work second front to match, reversing shapings.

Sleeves: (make 2) cast on 20 sts and work 2¾ ins (7 cm) in single rib. Change to garter st and work a further 6¼ ins (16 cm), increasing 1 stitch at each end of row 3 times, at regular intervals (26 sts).

Shape top of sleeve by decreasing 1 stitch at each end of alternate rows, on right side of work, 11 times, at the

White jacket

same time working raised patterns as follows: 7 sts in garter st, 1 st in st st, (4 sts in garter st, 1 st in st st) twice, 8 sts in garter st. Bind off remaining 4 sts.

Collar: join shoulder seams and pick up all sts around neck edge, with the exception of center front borders which will overlap. Work 2 ins (5 cm) in garter st, ending on wrong side of work. Now decrease 1 stitch at each end of next and alternate rows until 10 rows have been worked. Bind off all stitches fairly loosely.

Finishing: Join side seams. Sew up sleeve seams and set sleeves into armholes. Sew on buttons.

Light brown trousers

Materials: 4 skeins (1¾ oz/50 gr) sport weight yarn in light brown; 1 pr of no 6 needles: 1 cable needle.

Stitches used: stockinette stitch, single cable stitch (see page 92). These trousers are made in 2 pieces, with seams at center front, center back and inside legs.

Cast on 60 sts and work 13¾ ins (35 cm) in the following pattern: 28 sts in st st, 4 sts in single cable, 28 sts in st st. Lnd with a row on wrong side of work. Shape for crotch by increasing 1 stitch at each end of next, 3rd and 5th rows (66 sts). Keeping continuity of pattern, work nearly 8 ins (20 cm). Now change to single rib and work waistband. Bind off.

Make another piece to match.

Finishing: join leg seam of each

piece separately to a length of 15 ins (38 cm) from lower ege. Now join center fronts of both pieces together and then join center backs, to form upper part of trousers. Make a hem of about ¾ in (2 cm), or to suit height of child, all round lower edges.

Green trousers

Materials: 4 skeins (34 oz/100 gr) sport weight yarn; 1 pr of no 5 needles.
Stitches used: stockinette stitch, single rib (see page age 69).
Back: cast on 60 sts and work 13¾ ins (35 cm) in st st.
Continue for 1½ ins (4 cm), shaping

Green trousers

for crotch by increasing 1 stitch at each end of next 4 right side rows (68 sts).
Work a further 8 ins (20 cm) in st st, decreasing 1 stitch at each end of right side row 6 times (56 sts). Change to single rib and work a further 2 ins (2 cm).
Front: work exactly as for back.
Finishing: join leg seam of each piece separately to a length of 15¾ ins (40 cm) from lower edge. Now join center fronts of both pieces together and then join center backs, to form upper part of trousers. Make a hem of about 1 in (3 cm), or to suit height of child, all around lower edge.

White zip-front cardigan

Materials: 5 skeins (1¾ oz/50 gr) sport weight yarn; 1 pr of no 4 needles; 1 crochet hook size F/5; 15¾ ins (40 cm) separating zipper.
Stitches used: stockinette stitch and reversed stockinette st, double rib (see page 66), corded edge (see page 36). This cardigan is made all in one piece, starting from the back. Cast on 60 sts and work 2 ins (5 cm) in double rib. Continue straight for nearly 12 ins (30 cm).
Now make sleeves by casting on 60 sts at the beg of next 2 rows, working both rows in double rib. Still in double rib, work 4 ins (10 cm) on all 180 sts.
Bind off center 22 sts and working each side separately, continue for 2 ins (5 cm). Now cast on 6 sts at beg of next row to form front neck opening and continue, still in double rib, for 3⅛ ins (8 cm), working first 2 sts of each row at center front edge in r st st. Bind off 60 sts at beg of next row to complete sleeve and continue in st st for 12 ins (30 cm) continuing to work the first 2 sts of

Light brown trousers and white zip-front cardigan

each row at center front edge in r st st. Continue for 2 ins (5 cm) in double rib. Bind off. Complete second front. Finishing: with right side of work facing, pick up all sts down one of center front edges and work for 1½ ins (4 cm) in double rib. Bind off. Work second front edge to correspond. Now pick up all sts round neck opening, including those at ends of center front edgings just made, and work 1⅛ ins (3 cm) in double rib. Pick up all sts at end of one sleeve and work 1½ ins (4 cm) in double rib. Work on second sleeve to correspond. Join side and sleeve seams. With right side of work facing and using crochet hook, work a corded edge (see page 36) starting at lower corner of right center front and work-

ing up to top of neckband, all around neckband and down left center front, finishing off at lower corner. Work in the same way round both wrist edges. Sew in zipper.

White jerkin outlined in brown

Materials: 3 skeins (3½ oz/100 gr) worsted weight yarn in white and a small amount in brown; 1 pr of no 10½ needles; 1 crochet hook size K/10¼,

Stitches used: garter stitch, single crochet (see page 36). This jerkin is made in two pieces, starting from lower end of sleeves.

Cast on 14 sts and work 19¾ ins (50 cm) in garter st. Now increase for back by casting on 34 sts (48 sts) and continue for 12⅝ ins (32 cm) in garter st. Bind off the 34 sts previously cast on and continue on the remaining 14 sts for a further 19¾ ins (50 cm). Bind off.

Make a second piece, exactly the same, for front.

Pocket: cast on 12 sts and work 4¾ ins (42 cm) in garter st, to make a square.

Finishing: sew side, sleeve and shoulder seams, leaving a center opening 8 ins (20 cm) wide for neck. Stitch pocket near lower edge of front, on right-hand side, with lines of garter st running the same way as main fabric.

Using crochet hook and brown yarn, work a row of single crochet round edge of pocket, neck opening, wrists and along all seams, keeping stitches evenly spaced.

White jerkin outlined in brown

Red pullover with V-neck

Red pullover with V-neck

Materials: 4 skeins (3½ oz/100 gr) worsted weight yarn in red and small amounts in white and blue; 1 pr of no 7 needles; 1 set of double-pointed needles no 7.

Stitches used: garter stitch, reverse stockinette stitch, turban stitch (see page 90).

Back: cast on 33 sts and work 2 ins (5 cm) in garter st. Change to r st st and work 8⅝ ins (22 cm). Shape for armholes by binding off 2 sts at beg of next 2 rows (29 sts on needle) and continue for a further 5⅛ ins (13 cm) in r st st. Bind off.

Front: cast on 33 sts and work 2 ins (5 cm) in garter st. Change to turban st and work 7½ ins (19 cm). Now divide for V-neck opening by binding off center st and working each side separately, decreasing 1 stitch at neck edge on every right side row. When work in turban st measures 8⅝ ins (22 cm), shape for armhole by binding off 2 sts at beg of next armhole edge row. Keeping continuity of pattern, continue decreasing at neck edge until work measures the same as back. Bind off. Make second side to match, reversing shapings.

Sleeves: (make 2) cast on 20 sts and work 2 ins (5 cm) in garter st. Change to r st st and work 7 ins (18 cm), increasing 1 st at each end of row 6 times, at regular intervals. Shape top of sleeve by binding off 2 sts at beg of next 2 rows and then 1 stitch at each end of alternate rows until shaping measures the same as back and front armhole shapings.

Finishing: join side and shoulder

Light brown jacket

seams. Sew up sleeve seams and set sleeves into armholes. With double-pointed needles, pick up all stitches around V-neck opening and work in garter st as follows: 4 rows in red yarn, 2 rows in blue, 2 rows in white, 2 rows in red. Bind off fairly loosely.

Light brown jacket

Materials: 4 skeins (3½ oz/100 gr) worsted weight yarn in light brown; 1 pr of no 9 needles; 1 crochet hook size l/9; 6 buttons.
Stitches used: seed stitch (see page 76), grill stitch (see page 76), corded edge (see page 36).
Back: cast on 40 sts and work 2⅜ ins (6 cm) in seed st. Change to grill st and work 11 ins (28 cm). Shape for armhole by binding off 3 sts at beg of next 2 rows, 2 sts at beg of next 2 rows and 1 st at beg of next 2 rows (28 sts rem on needle). Continue straight for 6¼ ins (16 cm) and then bind off center 8 sts for neck shaping. Working each side separately, knit 2 rows in pattern and bind off.
Front half: cast on 23 sts and work 2⅜ ins (6 cm) in seed st. Continue for 11 ins (28 cm), working 17 sts in grill st and 6 sts in seed st. Shape armhole as for back.
Keeping continuity of pattern, work a further 5½ ins (14 cm), ending at center front. Bind off the border of 6 sts in seed st and 1 st from main fabric on next row. Continue until front half measures same as back. Bind off shoulder stitches. Make second front half to correspond.
NOTE: 6 buttonholes should be

Red tie-neck jacket

worked, spaced at regular intervals in either the right- or left-hand seed st border, according to whether the jacket is intended for a boy or a girl.

Sleeves: (make 2) cast on 22 sts and work 2⅜ ins (6cm) in seed st. Change to grill st and work a further 12 ins (30 cm), increasing 1 stitch at each end of row, at regular intervals, until there are 34 sts. Shape top of sleeve by binding off 3 sts at beg of next 2 rows, 2 sts at beg of next 2 rows and 1 stitch at beg of next 2 rows. Continue, decreasing at regular intervals at each end of row, until top of sleeve measures the same as armholes of front and back and 8 sts remain on the needle. Bind off.

Finishing: join side and shoulder seams. With right side of work facing, pick up all stitches round neck and work 2 rows in seed st. Continue for a further 8 rows, increasing 2 sts at beg of each row. Bind off. With crochet hook and using the yarn double, work a row of corded edge all round collar. Sew up sleeve seam and set sleeves into armholes. Sew on buttons.

Red tie-neck jacket

Materials: 4 skeins (1¾ oz/50 gr) mohair yarn in red; 1 pr of no 6 needles.

Stitches used: double rib (see page 66), stockinette stitch, reverse stockinette stitch.

Back: cast on 48 sts and work 11 ins (28 cm) in st st. Change to double rib and work a further 4 ins (10 cm). Now bind off center 14 sts and work each side separately, decreasing 1 stitch twice at neck edge, on right side of work. Bind off all sts for shoulders.

Half front: cast on 24 sts and work 11 ins (28 cm) in st st. Change to double rib and work a further 4 ins (10 cm). Bind off 8 sts at neck edge then decrease 1 stitch 6 times at neck edge, on right side of work. Bind off all sts for shoulder. Work second front the same way, reversing shapings.

Sleeves: (make 2) cast on 24 sts and work 3⅛ ins (8 cm) in double rib. Continue in st st for 10⅝ ins (27 cm). Bind off.

Finishing: join side seams as far as start of double ribbing; join shoulder seams; sew up sleeve seams and set sleeves into armholes.

Turn in 1½ ins (4 cm) all along lower edge and stitch neatly into place to form a hem.

To make the front borders, cast on 8 sts and work in r st st for 13¾ ins (35 cm). Bind off. Work a second strip. Fold each strip in half, lengthwise, purl side outwards, and stitch neatly to center fronts with a flat seam.

To make neck band and ties, cast on 8 sts and work in r st st for 41½ ins (105 cm). Fold in half lengthwise, establish center and sew from center back of neck to top of center front borders with a flat seam. This should leave about 12 ins (30 cm) free on each side to tie at neck.

White hooded jerkin

Materials: 3 skeins (3½ oz/100 gr) worsted weight yarn in white; 1 pr of no 10½ needles; 2 spare needles in same size; 1 wooden toggle.

Stitches used: stockinette stitch, garter stitch.

Back: cast on 38 sts and work 1½ ins (4 cm) in garter st. Continue for 9⅞ ins (25 cm) in st st and then begin decreasing for raglan shoulder (see page 45) until shaping measures 6 ins (15 cm) and 12 sts remain. Do not bind off but leave these sts on a spare needle.

Front: cast on 38 sts and work 1½ ins (4 cm) in garter st. Continue for 7 ins (18 cm) in st st, ending with a row on right side of work. On next row, purl 18 sts, knit next 2 sts, purl 18 sts. Continue working straight, increasing knitted stitches by 2 at center of each purl row as follows: p17, k4, p17; p16, k6, p16; p15, k8, p15. This will give a garter stitch design at center on right side of work.

Now divide for center front opening by working on each half of the stitches separately, retaining the border of 4 sts in garter stitch throughout and at the same time decreasing for raglan shaping until work measures same as back and 6 sts remain on needle (4 border sts and 2 armhole sts). Leave these stitches on a spare needle.

Sleeves: (make 2) cast on 25 sts and work 1½ ins (4 cm) in garter st. Continue for a further 9⅞ ins (25 cm) in st st, then begin decreasing for raglan shoulder shaping until only 2 central sts and 6 side sts remain. Leave these sts on a spare needle.

Finishing: with right side of work facing, pick up all the stitches from top of r front, sleeve, back, sleeve, l front and work 12 ins (30 cm) in garter st. Bind off. Fold this piece of knitting in half, wrong sides together, and join bound off edge to form hood. Join side and sleeve seams and sew raglan sleeves to front and back with a flat seam. Sew toggle on one garter st border; make a loop on the other to correspond.

Pockets: (make 2) cast on 10 sts and work 2 ins (5 cm) in st st and a further 1⅜ ins (3.5 cm) in garter st. Position the two pockets just above garter st

White hooded jerkin

border at lower front edge and about 2 ins (5 cm) away from side seams. Sew neatly into place.

3-color sweater

Materials: 1 skein (1¾ oz/50 gr) sport weight yarn in white; and ½ skein each in blue and red; 1 pr of no 2 needles; 1 crochet hook size B/1; 4 small buttons.

Stitches used: stockinette stitch, single rib (see page 69), single crochet, corded edge (see page 36).

Back: using white yarn, cast on 92 sts and work ¾ in (2 cm) in single rib. Still using white yarn, change to st st and work 7 rows. Now introduce the blue yarn and work 1 stitch blue, 1 stitch white for entire row. On return row, work white on white and blue on blue. For next row, work white on blue and blue on white and work return row as before. Using white yarn, work 5 rows in st st. Now start second band of pattern by introducing red yarn and working as follows: 2 sts in white, 1 st in red for entire row. Return row, work white on white and red on red. On next row, move each red st to the left. Return row, as before. On next row, move each red st to the left again. Return row as before. Work 5 rows, using white yarn, in st st.

Repeat these 11 rows, alternating bands of red and blue, until work measures 6¼ ins (16 cm) from start. When work measures 5½ ins (14 cm), however, start shaping for armholes by decreasing 2 sts at each end of every knit row 4 times.

At 6¼ ins (16 cm), divide for back

189

3-color sweater and red skirt

opening by working on half the stitches until work measures 9½ ins (24 cm). Still keeping continuity of 2-color pattern, bind off 10 sts twice at shoulder edge and bind off remaining stitches. Work other side of back opening to correspond.

Front: using white yarn, cast on 92 sts and work ¾ in (2 cm) in single rib. Change to st st and, after working 7 rows with white yarn, introduce blue yarn and work as for back. When 5½ ins (14 cm) have been worked, shape for armholes by decreasing 2 sts at each end of every knit row 4 times.

When work measures 9 ins (23 cm) from start, bind off central 16 sts and work each side separately, decreas-ing 1 stitch at neck edge of every knit row, until same length as back. Shape each shoulder as for back.

Sleeves: (make 2) using white yarn, cast on 50 sts and work ½ in (1.5 cm) in single rib. Change to st st and work 7 rows. Continue in pattern as for back, introducing contrasting col-ors in the same order, increasing 1 stitch 7 times at each end of right side row (64 sts). Matching bands of pattern with front and back, shape armholes as for back, continuing to dec 1 st at each end of every knit row until work measures 6¼ ins (16 cm). Bind off.

Finishing: join side and shoulder seams; sew up sleeve seams and set sleeves into armholes. With right side of work facing, pick up all sts around neck opening and work in single rib, 2 rows in red yarn, 2 rows in white and 2 rows in blue. Bind off by using the tubular method.

To finish off back neck opening, using white yarn, work 2 rows of sc (making 4 buttonholes at regular intervals on one side) and one row of corded edge on both sides. Sew on buttons.

Red skirt

Materials: 4 skeins (3½ oz/100 gr) of sport weight yarn in red; 1 pr of no 6 needles; 1 pr of no 2 needles.

Stitches used: single rib (see page 69), English rib (see page 66).

Using no 6 needles, cast on 82 sts and work 9½ ins (24 cm) in English rib. Change to no 2 needles and continue for 2¾ ins (7 crn) in single rib. Work a second piece in exactly the same way.

Finishing: join side seams.

White skirt with shoulder straps

Materials: 3 skeins (3½ oz/100 gr) of worsted weight yarn in white; 1 pr of no 6 needles; 1 spare needle; 1 set of double-pointed no 4 needles; 2 buttons.

Stitches used: reversed stockinette stitch, single rib (see page 69).

This little skirt consists of four identical panels made as follows: using no 6 needles, cast on 46 sts and work 15 ins (38 cm) in r st st, decreasing at each end of row, at regular intervals, until 26 sts remain. Leave these sts on spare needle and work 3 more panels in the same way.

Finishing: using set of double-pointed needles, divide all the sts between 3 needles and work 2 ins (5 cm) in single rib. Bind off.

Join panel seams, making them as flat as possible near ribbing. Turn in 1½ ins (4 cm) all round on lower edge and stitch neatly into place to form a hem.

Now make straps by casting on 12 sts and working 17½ ins (44 cm) in single rib. Make a loop at one end. Make another identical strap. For cross strap, cast on 12 sts and work 4¾ ins (12 cm). Bind off. Stitch the long straps to center top front of skirt, 2¾ ins (7 cm) apart, and sew the short strap to inner edges of both straps about 2 ins (5 cm) from skirt top. Sew buttons to center top back, 2¾ ins (7 cm) apart.

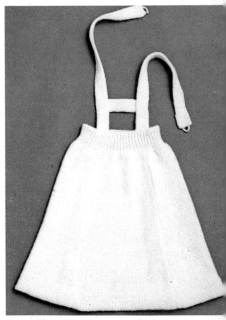

White skirt with shoulder straps

Yellow dress

Materials: 5 skeins (1¾ oz/50 gr) of sport weight yarn in yellow and a little dark blue; a small quantity of turquoise and red yarn for embroidery; 1 pr of no 6 needles; 1 pr of no 4 needles; 1 set of double-pointed no 4 needles.

Stitches used: stockinette stitch and reversed stockinette st, single rib (see page 69).

Back: using no 6 needles, cast on 90 sts and work 12 ins (30 cm) in st st. Change to no 4 needles and work 2⅜ ins (4 cm) in single rib. Change back to no 6 needles and work a further 4¾ ins (12 cm) in st st. To shape for armholes, decrease 3 sts at each end of next 2 knit rows and 2 sts at each end of next knit row.

Continue straight for 4¾ ins (12 cm). Now bind off central 24 sts and work ¾ in (2 cm) on each side separately. Bind off.

Front: using no 6 needles, cast on 90 sts and work in following pattern for 12 ins (30 cm): 24 sts in st st, 11 sts in r st st, 19 sts in st st, 11 sts in r st st, 25 sts in st st. Change to no 4 needles and work 2⅜ ins (6 cm) in single rib. Change back to no 6 needles and work a further 4¾ ins (12 cm) in st st. To shape for armholes, decrease as follows: next 2 rows, bind off 6 sts at beg of each row; on next 3 knit rows decrease 3 sts, 2 sts and 2 sts at each end of needle.

Neck opening: divide work in half by binding off central 6 sts and continue each side separately. Decreasing 2 sts at neck edge, continue in st st for another 4 ins (10 cm). Bind off.

Finishing: join side and shoulder seams. Turn in 1 in (3 cm) all around lower edge for hem and stitch neatly into place. With double-pointed needles, pick up all sts around neck edge and work ¾ in (2 cm) in single rib. Bind off fairly loosely. Work in exactly the same way around both armholes.

Embroider a little floral motif at center front, using turquoise and red yarn, allowing background yellow to show through center of flowers.

Make a twisted cord (see page 56) with the dark blue yarn and thread through center of waist ribbing.

Yellow dress

Blue overalls

Materials: 3 skeins (3½ oz/100 gr) of worsted weight yarn in blue; 1 pr of no 6 needles; 1 spare needle; 1 crochet hook; 6 buttons.

Stitches used: stockinette stitch and reversed stockinette st, crocheted chain.

Back: cast on 30 sts and work 12¼ ins (31 cm) in r st st, ending with a knit row. On next row, inc 1 st on right edge of work, purl to end of row. Rep this inc on foll 3 purl rows (4 sts increased altogether). Leave sts on a spare needle.

Work another piece in same way, but working the increases on left edge.

Replace all sts onto one needle, with increases at center (these will form the crotch). Continue for 6¼ ins (16 cm) in r st st. Now work 2¾ ins (7 cm) in st st, then 3 rows in r st st, and another 2 ins (5 cm) in st st. Shape for armholes by binding off 3 sts at beg of next 2 rows and continue in st st for a further ¾ in (2 cm). Work next 3 rows in r st st, then another 2⅜ ins (6 cm) in st st. Bind off central 20 sts for neck opening and work on each side separately as follows: 3 rows in r st st, 2⅜ ins (6 cm) in st st, 3 rows in r st st. 1⅛ in (3 cm) in st st. Bind off.

Front: work exactly as for back.

Finishing: join side and inside leg seams. Turn in ¾ in (2 cm) all around lower edge of trousers and stitch neatly into place to form hem. With right side of work facing, pick up all stitches along edges of front neck opening and work 1⅜ ins (3.5 cm) in r st st. Work in same way at back neck opening and all round both armholes. Fold these bands in half, inwards, and stitch neatly into place.

With crochet hook, work 2 lengths of chain to equal width of shoulder straps and stitch down in 4 places, on top edge of front straps, to form 3 loops on each. Sew buttons to correspond on back straps.

Blue overalls

Now introduce the 3 contrasting colors for train design (see diagram no 6 on pages 132–133) as shown in illustration. Work a further 6¼ ins (16 cm) in st st and then bind off 2 center sts. Continue in st st, working each side separately, as follows: decrease 1 st every 2 rows at neck edge and, at the same time, shape armhole as for back. When front measures same as back, bind off shoulder sts.

Finishing: join side and shoulder seams. Using double-pointed needles (see page 20), pick up all sts evenly round V-neck edge and work ⅜ in (1 cm) in single rib. Bind off fairly loosely. Pick up all sts around each armhole and work ⅜ in (1 cm) in single rib. Bind off.

Light blue sleeveless pullover
Light blue sleeveless pullover

Materials: 2 skeins (1¾ oz/50 gr) of sport weight yarn in light blue and a little dark blue, yellow and red; 1 pr of no 2 needles; 1 set of double-pointed no 2 needles.

Stitches used: single rib (see page 69), stockinette stitch.

Back: cast on 56 sts and work 1½ ins (4 cm) in single rib; change to st st and work 10¼ ins (26 cm) ending with a purl row. Now shape for armholes by binding off 3 sts at beg of next 2 rows and then decreasing 2 sts at each end of next 2 knit rows. Continue straight for a further 4 ins (10 cm). Shape shoulders by binding off 7 sts at beg of next 2 rows. Bind off all remaining sts.

Front: cast on 56 sts and work 1½ ins (4 cm) in single rib; change to st st and work ¾ in (2 cm) in st st.

For babies and toddlers

This chapter is devoted to garments for the youngest member of the family. While the first layette is usually made by caring relatives and friends before the baby arrives, there are so many things that can be made at home – crib and carriage coverlets, outdoor clothes, etc. – which give that touch of individuality and express the mother's personal taste. Just one word of advice – always use yarns that are soft and smooth when making anything for babies and small children. Anything scratchy or fluffy may cause irritation or breathing problems.

White coat

Materials: 6 skeins (1¾ oz/50 gr) of sport or baby yarn in white; 1 pr of no 1 needles; 1 spare needle; 1 crochet hook size B/1; 8 mother-of-pearl buttons.

Stitches used: stockinette stitch, single rib (see page 69), single crochet, corded edge (see page 36).

Back: (skirt is worked in 2 pieces) cast on 70 sts and work 9⅞ ins (25 cm) in st st, decreasing 5 sts at regular intervals on right edge and ending on left (straight edge) of work. Leave sts on spare needle.

Make a second piece to match, with decreasing worked on left edge, and ensure that last row ends on left edge. Now work next row in single rib to last 20 sts, place stitches held on spare needle over work in hand and knit 1 st from front needle with 1 st from back needle (i.e. the last 20 sts from side with left-edge decreases are worked together with first 20 sts from side with right-edge decreases – straight sides overlapping, shaped sides at outside edges). There should now be 110 sts on needle. Continue to work straight for 2⅜ ins (6 cm), still in single rib, ending with a row on wrong side of work. Now shape for armholes by decreasing 2 sts at each end of next

and following 6 rows on right side of work (82 sts remain). Continue in single rib for a further 2¾ ins (7 cm). Shape shoulders by binding off 7 sts at beg of next 6 rows. Bind off remaining 40 sts.

Left front: cast on 70 sts and work 9⅞ ins (25 cm) in st st, decreasing 5 sts at regular intervals on left edge and ending on left (shaped) edge of work. Continue for 2⅜ ins (6 cm), working first 40 sts of next row in single rib and remaining 25 sts in st st and return row as sts appear on needle. End with a return row. Now shape for armhole by decreasing 2 sts at beg of next and following 6 rows on right side of work (51 sts rem). Continue in pattern for 2⅜ ins (6 cm), ending at center front. For neck shaping, bind off 13 sts from center front and continue decreasing 2 sts at neck edge on right side of work until left front measures same as back (21 sts rem).

Shape shoulders by binding off 7 sts at beg of next 3 rows at armhole edge.

Right front: work as for left front, reversing shapings and pattern.

Sleeves: (make 2) cast on 56 sts and work 7 ins (18 cm) in single rib, increasing 1 st at each end of row 5 times, at regular intervals. Now shape top of sleeve, still working in

White coat

single rib, by decreasing 2 sts at each of next and every alternate row, until sleeve measures 9½ ins (24 cm) from start.

Finishing: join side and shoulder seams; sew up sleeve seams and set sleeves into armholes. With right side of work facing, cross one side over the other (which way will depend upon whether coat is intended for a boy or girl) and mark a point approximately half-way across st st panels on left and right fronts. Starting from point marked on right front, pick up all sts around neck edge until point marked on left front. Work 2 ins (5 cm) in single rib, increasing 1 st on next to last st at each end of row 8 times, at regular intervals. Bind off fairly loosely.

To make belt, which is in 2 parts, pick up 10 sts along the line on each Front where st st meets single rib and work each piece in single rib until it reaches a little more than half-way around back of coat. Bind off. Stitch ends in position neatly and sew 2 buttons about ¾ in (2 cm) each side of center.

Turn in about 2 ins (5 cm) of lower edge of coat and stitch neatly into place to form hem.

Using crochet hook, work 1 row of sc and 1 row of corded edge all round edges as follows: (with right side of work facing), start at lower corner of center right front and work to top corner, along neck opening, all round edges of collar and 2nd neck opening and down center left front, making 3 button loops in crocheted chain at regular intervals, during the sc row, between neck edge and waist, on one side only. Work same edging round both wrists.

Sew on buttons to correspond with buttonhole loops and 3 more buttons on same st st panel as that on which buttonhole loops have been worked, for double-breasted effect.

White and pink sweater and bootees

Sweater. Materials: 1 skein (1¾ oz/50 gr) of sport or baby yarn in white and a little pink; 5 tiny buttons; 1 pr of no 2 needles; 2 spare needles.

Stitches used: stockinette stitch, seed stitch (see page 76), single rib (see page 69), garter stitch.

This little sweater is worked in one piece, starting from neck edge.

Cast on 104 sts by the tubular method and work 10 rows in same method. In next row, work 20 sts in st st (for half Back), inc 1 stitch (this to be a single internal between-stitch increase: see page 30) k1 and inc 1 stitch, for openwork effect raglan shaping. Now work 15 sts (for sleeve), inc 1, k1, inc 1, as before. Work 30 sts (for front), inc 1, k1, inc 1 as before. Work 15 sts (for second sleeve), inc 1, k1, inc 1 as before. Work last 20 sts (second half back). Knitting first and last 7 sts, purl return row (112 sts). Third row: k 7 for garter st border, k 14, inc for corner as above, k 17, inc for corner, k 32, inc for corner, k 17, inc for corner, k 14, k 7 for border. Knitting first and last 7 sts, purl return row (120 sts). Keeping the first and last 7 sts of each row in garter st to form borders for back opening, and making 5 baby clothes buttonholes (see page 41) at regular intervals on one side, continue as above, increasing 2 sts on each side of central stitch at each corner on right side rows and incorporating new sts into st st. Return rows are purled (except for borders).

When 2 ins (5 cm) have been worked from start, introduce pink yarn and work 5 rows in seed st. With white yarn, continue for a further 1½ ins (4 cm) working as above and then, with pink yarn, work

White and pink sweater and bootees

another 5 rows in seed st.

When work measures 4¾ ins (12 cm) from start, the no of stitches on needle should be: 46 for each of the two half backs, 69 for each sleeve and 82 for the front (312 sts, in all).

Leave the two sets of sleeve sts on 2 spare needles and continue working in white yarn on the two half backs and the front for another 4¾ ins (12 cm) in st st. Work another ¾ in in seed st, still in white yarn, and bind off fairly loosely.

Return to sts left on one of the spare needles and continue in white yarn, working sleeve in st st, at the same time decreasing 1 stitch at each end of row 12 times, at regular intervals, until 45 sts remain. Change to single rib and work 1⅜ ins (3.5 cm). Bind off. Return to second set of sts and make another sleeve to match.

Finishing: join side and sleeve seams. Sew on buttons to correspond with buttonholes.

Bootees. Materials: ½ oz (15 gr) of sport or baby yarn in white and a little pink; a length of green yarn; 1 pr of no 4 needles; 2 spare needles (optional).

Stitches used: stockinette stitch and reversed stockinette st, single rib (see page 69).

Using white yarn, cast on 40 sts and work in single rib as follows: ¾ in (2 cm), change to pink yarn for 2 rows, then ½ in (1.5 cm) in white, 2 rows in pink, ¾ in (2 cm) in white. Still with white yarn, work 2 rows in st st and then 1 row as follows: *k1, yo, k2 tog * to make holes for cords. Continue in r st st for 4 rows.

Working only on center 14 sts (the 13 sts on each side can either be slipped onto 2 short spare needles or onto a length of yarn), proceed as follows: 16 rows in st st, 4 rows in r st st, 4 rows in st st, 4 rows in r st st.

Return to 13 sts on spare needle (or yarn) at left edge of work, pick up 14 sts from left edge of knitting just worked (instep); work across the center 14 sts, pick up 14 sts from right edge of instep and continue across 13 sts on right side of work (68 sts altogether). Work 4 rows in st st and 4 rows in r st st. Rep these 8 rows once more.

To form the sole, in st st, work first two and last two sts together and decrease center 14 sts on both knit and purl rows (i.e. on right and wrong side of work) until they have all been eliminated. Twenty-two sts will be left on each side. Bind off.

Work another bootee in exactly the same way.

To make up and complete: sew up back and seam along sole so that joins are invisible. Embroider a small flower and leaves with the pink yarn and a length of green yarn on the front of each bootee. Make 2 looped cords (see page 56) and thread through holes on each bootee.

Pram outfit with squirrel motif

Sweater. Materials: approx 2 skeins (1¾ oz/50 gr) of sport or baby yarn in main color and small amounts in mid-brown, light brown, orange and dark brown; 1 pr of no 2 needles; 6 small buttons.

Stitches used: stockinette stitch and reversed stockinette st, mock English rib (see page 66), garter stitch.

Left back: cast on 40 sts and work for 5½ ins (14 cm) in mock English rib, except for the first 8 sts of every row which are worked in garter st as border for back opening in which 6 horizontal buttonholes (see page 40) should be worked, at regular intervals, as work progresses. (These may be worked on right back, if

Pram outfit with squirrel motif

preferred.)

Shape for raglan armhole (see page 45), working in st st but retaining the 8 border sts in garter st. Continue until 19 sts remain and work measures 10¼ ins (26 cm). Bind off.

Right back: work same, reversing shapings.

Front: cast on 72 sts and work 5½ ins (14 cm) in mock English rib.

Now change to st st and shape for raglan armhole, at the same time following diagram no 3 (see page 131).

When work measures 9⅞ ins (25 cm), cast off center 18 sts and work each side separately, continuing to decrease a further 6 sts at raglan shoulder edge, when work should measure the same as back. Bind off.

Sleeves: (make 2) cast on 38 sts and

work 1¾ ins (4.5 cm) in mock English rib. Change to st st (except for the first and last 2 sts of every row which should be worked in garter st), increasing 1 st at each end of row 12 times, at regular intervals, until there are 62 sts on needle and work measures 6 ins (15 cm). Now decrease for raglan shoulder until 6 sts remain and work measures 11 ins (28 cm). Bind off.

Finishing: join side and sleeve seams. Starting from top center corner of left back, pick up all sts along left back, sleeve, front, sleeve and right back. Work 4 rows in garter st, 2 rows in st st and 3 rows in r st st. Bind off fairly loosely.

Pants. Materials: 1 skein of sport weight yarn in mid-brown; 1 pr of no 5 needles; 1 crochet hook size E/4.

Stitches used: single rib (see page 69), stockinette stitch, single crochet, corded edge (see page 36).

Back: cast on 40 sts and work 1⅛ ins (3 cm) in single rib; continue for 4¾ ins (12 cm) in st st. Now bind off 5 sts at beg of next 4 rows and 6 sts at beg of next 2 rows (bind off as if to knit on knit rows and as if to purl on purl rows). Bind off remaining center 8 sts.

Front: work exactly the same as back.

Finishing: join side seams and center 8 sts to form crotch. Using crotchet hook, work 1 round of sc and 1 round of corded edge all around lower edges of trousers.

Helmet. Materials: 1 skein in main colour; 1 pr of no 2 needles; 1 spare needle; 1 button.

Stitches used: stockinette stitch, garter stitch.

The earflaps are the first things to be worked: cast on 6 sts and work ⅜ in (1 cm) in garter st. Now make a 2 st horizontal buttonhole (see page 40) and continue in garter st for another 2⅛ ins (5.5. cm). Work 1 row as follows: 2 sts in garter st, 2 sts in st st, 2 sts in garter st. Keeping borders in garter st, increase 1 st at each side of center stitches on every knit row until there are 22 sts on needle.

Now cast on 12 sts on right edge of earflap and work as follows for ⅜ in (1 cm): 2 sts in st st, 10 sts in garter st and, at the same time, continue to work left part as before (2 sts in garter st, st st to last 2 sts, 2 sts in garter st) without further increases. Continue working on right side for 4 ins (10 cm): 2 sts in st st, 2 sts in garter st and the rest in st st. Leave sts on spare needle.

Cast on 6 sts and work ⅜ in (1 cm) in garter st. Continue as for first earflap, increasing at both sides as before until work measures 2 ins (5 cm).

Now cast on 12 sts on left of earflap and continue as previously, continuing on right without increasing further until work measures 4 ins (10 cm).

At this point, starting from the cast-on sts on left side of second earflap, cast on another 30 sts and continue across first earflap and the other sts cast on at right side of first earflap. Working the other sts as they are on needle, work the 30 sts just cast on as follows: 6 rows in garter st, then: 2 sts in st st, 2 sts in garter st, 22 sts in st st, 2 sts in garter st, 2 sts in st st. Continue in this way for 3⅛ ins (8 cm).

Now begin decreasing 1 stitch at each side of panels formed by the 2 sts in st st, working all the other sts in garter st. Continue in this way until 1 st remains. Fasten off.

To make up and complete: join helmet at the side. Make a pompon (see page 55) and stitch it firmly to top of helmet. Sew button onto right earflap to correspond with buttonhole.

Bootees. Materials: ½ skein in main

color; 1 pr of no 2 needles; 2 short spare needles (optional); 1 crochet hook.

Stitches used: stockinette stitch and reversed stockinette st, crocheted chain.

Cast on 48 sts and work 2 rows in plain st st and 2 rows in r st st. Continue for ⅜ ins (1 cm) in st st, ending with a purl row. Now work a row of holes for cord as follows: *k2, yo, k2 tog*. Work a purl row. Leave 18 sts from each side on a piece of yarn (or on 2 spare needles) and work 1½ ins (4 cm) in st st on the 12 center sts, ending with a purl row. Return to sts at left edge of work and work them; pick up and knit 12 sts along instep; knit the 12 center sts; pick up and knit 12 sts from second instep and work across the 18 sts left on spare needle.

Work 2 rows in r st st, 2 rows in st st and another 2 rows in r st st. Continue in st st for a further 1⅛ ins (3 cm) to form the sole. Bind off. Work second bootee.

Finishing: sew up back of bootee and sew up sole invisibly with duplicate stitch (see page 58). Make 2 lengths of crocheted chain and thread them through the little holes, starting and ending at center front. Make 4 small tassels (see page 54) and attach them to cord ends.

4-piece outfit in white and blue
(See illustration on page 203)

Top. Materials: 1 skein (1¾ oz/50 gr) of sport or baby yarn in white and one in blue; 1 pr of no 5 needles; 1 set of double-pointed no 5 needles; 2 spare needles; 1 crochet hook size F/5.

Stitches used: garter stitch, single rib (see page 69), honeycomb stitch (see page 78), single crochet, corded edge (see page 36), crocheted chain.

Half back: using white yarn, cast on 18 sts and work 1½ ins (4 cm) in single rib. Continue for 4¾ ins (12 cm) in garter st. Leave sts on spare needle. Work second half in exactly the same way.

Front: cast on 30 sts and work 1½ ins (4 cm) in single rib. Continue for 4¾ ins (12 cm) in garter st. Leave sts on spare needle.

Sleeves: (make 2) cast on 24 sts and work 1⅜ ins (3.5 cm) in single rib. Now work a row of holes for wrist cord as follows: *k2, yo, k2 tog*. Continue for 5⅛ ins (13 cm) in garter st, increasing 1 stitch at each end of row 4 times, at regular intervals. When required length is reached, leave these 32 sts on spare needle.

For yoke, introduce blue wool and with right side of work facing, work first row of honeycomb st across all the stitches from one of the half backs, then from one of the sleeves, the front, the other sleeve and the second half back. Continue in honeycomb st, decreasing regularly until 56 sts remain. Now change to white yarn and work another 2 rows, decreasing 10 sts at regular intervals all around on both rows. Cast off remaining 36 sts fairly loosely.

Finishing: join side and sleeve seams. Using white yarn and crochet hook, work a row of sc up right center back edge, around neck opening and down left center back edge. Change to blue yarn and work a corded edge. Work 2 lengths of crocheted chain, using double yarn (1 white and 1 blue); thread through holes at wrists.

Pants. Materials: 1 skein yarn in white and a little in blue; 1 pr of no 5 needles; 1 crochet hook size F/5.

Stitches used: single rib (see page 69), garter stitch, single crochet, corded edge (see page 36).

Back: cast on 36 sts and work 1⅛ ins (3 cm) in single rib. Continue for 6 ins (15 cm) in garter st. Shape crotch by increasing 1 stitch on each side of central stitch 6 times. Bind off these increased sts and continue working each side separately in garter st for a further 1½ ins (4 cm). Bind off.

Front: work exactly the same as back.

Finishing: join side seams; join inside leg and crotch seams. Using white yarn and crochet hook, work a row of sc around lower edge of both legs; change to blue yarn and work a row of corded edge. Work a length of crocheted chain, using double yarn (1 white and 1 blue); thread it through between end of ribbing and beginning of garter st.

Bootees. Materials: small amount in white and blue; 1 pr of no 6 needles; 2 short spare needles (optional); 1 crochet hook size F/5.

Stitches used: single rib (see page 69), stockinette stitch, garter stitch.

Using white yarn, cast on 27 sts and work 2 ins (5 cm) in single rib. Now work a row of holes for cord as follows: *k2, yo, k2 tog*. Work 1 row in st st. Leave first and last 9 sts on spare needle (or on a length of yarn) and work on center 9 sts for 1½ ins (4 cm), alternating white and blue yarn every 4 rows.

Now work the 9 sts from left edge, pick up and work (in garter st) 9 sts along the instep, work the 9 center sts, pick up and work (in garter st) 9 sts along other edge of instep and then work the 9 sts from right edge. Continue in garter st for 10 rows. Bind off.

Work second bootee in exactly the same way.

Finishing: join back seam of bootees and stitch sole together as invisibly as possible.

Using crochet hook and double yarn (1 white and 1 blue), make 2 crocheted chain cords and thread through holes.

Mitts. Materials: small amounts (less than 1 oz) of yarn in white and blue; 1 pr of no 5 needles; 1 crochet hook size F/5.

Stitches used: single rib (see page 69), garter stitch.

Cast on 24 sts and work 1⅛ ins (3 cm) in single rib. Now work a row of holes for wrist cord as follows: *k2, yo, k2 tog*. Change to garter st, alternating 4 rows in white yarn and 4 rows in blue, 4 times.

Shape top by knitting 2 sts tog on following rows until 1 st remains. Finish off.

Make second mitt in exactly the same way.

Finishing: join side seam, matching bands of color. With crochet hook and double yarn (1 strand of blue and 1 of white), work 2 lengths of crocheted chain and thread through wrist holes.

White overalls for the new baby
(See illustration on page 205)

Materials: 2 skeins (1¾ oz/50 gr) of sport or baby yarn in white and a little pink; 1 pr of no 1 needles; 2 spare needles; 2 small buttons.

Stitches used: garter stitch, stockinette stitch and reversed stockinette st, single rib (see page 69), seed stitch (see page 76).

Back: this is started from the top, at the loose end of the straps. Cast on 9 sts and work 4¾ ins (12 cm). Leave sts on spare needle. Work a 2nd strap in the same way. At end of last row, turn work, cast on 25 sts and work across the 9 sts of first strap (43 sts on needle). Continue in garter st for ½ in (1.5 cm) and then change to following pattern: 5 sts in garter

4-piece outfit in white and blue

st, 33 sts in st st, 5 sts in garter st, increasing on first and last stitch in st st, until there are 80 sts on needle and work measures 3½ ins (9 cm).

Now work 1 in (2.5 cm) in single rib and then change to st st for 5½ ins (14 cm), ending on a purl row.

Divide for legs by working first 40 sts leaving remaining 40 sts on spare needle. Work each leg separately, gradually decreasing at inside leg edge until 25 sts remain and 7 ins (18 cm) have been worked from division. Work the other leg to correspond. Leave sts of both legs on spare needle.

Front: cast on 45 sts and work top border of ½ in (1.5 cm) in garter st, making a 1 stitch buttonhole (see page 41) at each end of border at the same distance from outer edges. Continue in pattern as follows: 5 sts in garter st, 2 sts in st st, 1 st in seed st, 9 sts in st st, 1 st in seed st, 9 sts in st st, 1 st in seed st, 9 sts in st st, 1 st in seed st, 2 sts in st st, 5 sts in garter st. Keeping continuity of pattern with 4 vertical lines of seed st and outside borders of 5 garter sts, increase 1 stitch on first and last st st of next 8 rows, the last of which should be on wrong side of work. Work 9th row as follows: 10 sts in garter st, 6 sts in st st, 30 sts in r st st, 5 sts in st st, 10 sts in garter st.

Still increasing on first and last stitches on alternate rows in st st, continue as before for 12 rows, retaining garter st borders and the 3 st st panels separated by vertical seed st lines.

Now work 13th row as for previous 9th row, retaining center panel of 30 sts in r st st, and adjusting outer panels to include extra sts.

Work a further 12 rows, as before, but discontinue increasing when there are 79 sts on needle and increase one st at center front on 12th row (80 sts).

Continue exactly as for back, from waist ribbing until both legs have been worked and all sts are on a spare needle. With right side of work facing and starting with sts of one of the back legs, work in single rib across back and front sts for 1⅛ ins (3 cm). Leaving sts on each side of center 11 sts either on spare needles or threaded onto a length of yarn, work on the center 11 sts for 1⅜ ins (3.5 cm) in st st. Break off yarn. Still in st st, work across sts on spare needle to left, pick up and knit 11 sts along edge of instep just worked, knit across the 11 center sts, pick up and knit 11 sts along other edge of instep and work across sts on right needle.

Work 2 rows in r st st, 2 rows in st st, 2 rows in r st st, 2 rows in st st, 1 row in r st st and finish with ¾ in (2 cm) in st st.

Finishing: join side and inside leg seams; sew up back and soles of feet with flat seams and invisible stitches. Using the pink yarn, embroider a few stitches in the middle of the squares formed by seed st and r st st lines and sew buttons to end of straps to coincide with buttonholes worked at each side of top front border.

Beige and green sweater
(See illustration on page 206)

Materials: 1 skein (1¾ oz/50 gr) of sport or baby yarn in beige and 1 skein in green; small amounts in yellow, light brown and black; 1 pr of no 2 needles; 6 small buttons.

Stitches used: stockinette stitch, single rib (see page 69), double rib (see page 66).

Half back: using green yarn, cast on 46 sts and work 4 ins (10 cm) in double rib but working 8 sts on one side (which will form border of back opening) in single rib throughout. Change to beige yarn and work 4 rows in st st and then 2 rows in green yarn, still retaining the 8 st single rib border on one side. With beige yarn, work another 1⅜ ins (3.5 cm).

Now decrease for raglan shoulder (see page 45) until 20 sts remain and shaping measures 10⅝ ins (27 cm). Bind off.

Work another piece to correspond, with shaping and opening border on opposite sides. On one of the two single rib borders, 6 single stitch buttonholes (see page 41) should be worked, at regular intervals.

Front: using green yarn, cast on 84 sts and work 4 ins (10 cm) in double rib. Change to beige yarn and work 4 rows in st st and then 2 rows in green yarn. Now follow diagram no 9 (see page 132) for a further 2 ins (5 cm) and then start decreasing for raglan shoulder. When this measures 8⅝ ins (22 cm), bind off center 18 sts. Work each piece separately, continuing to decrease for raglan shoulder and, at the same time, binding off 1 stitch at neck edge of every knit row until 1 st remains. Fasten off.

Sleeves: (make 2) using green yarn, cast on 50 sts and work 4 ins (10 cm) in double rib. Change to beige yarn and work 4 rows in st st and then 2 rows in green yarn. Continue in beige yarn, increasing at each end of row at regular intervals until there are 62 sts on needle and 2½ ins (6.5 cm) have been worked in beige. Now decrese for raglan shaping as for back until 4 sts remain. Bind off.

Finishing: join side and sleeve seams. Join front and back to sleeves with a flat seam. Using green yarn pick up all the stitches evenly round neck opening and work 2 rows in garter st; change to beige yarn and work another 5 rows in single rib.

Bind off by the tubular method. Sew on the buttons to correspond with buttonholes worked in single rib border of one of the half backs.

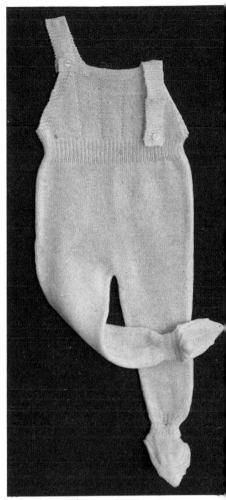

White overalls for the new baby

Bonnet, bootees and mitts in 2 colors

Bonnet. Materials: 1 oz/29 gr of fingering or baby yarn in first color and a small amount in second color; 1 pr of no 5 needles; 1 crochet hook size F/5.

Stitches used: garter stitch, stockinette stitch, crocheted chain.

Using main color, cast on 45 sts and work 4 rows in garter st, change to second color and work 2 rows and then a further 2 rows in first color. Still in main color, work 3⅛ ins (8 cm) in st st, ending with a purl row.

Next row, work on center 15 sts in st st, incorporating one stitch from side panel on each row as follows: on every row on right side of work, slip last st of center panel to right needle, k first stitch from side panel, pass slipped stitch over, turn; on every row on wrong side of work, purl last st of center panel together with first stitch from side panel, turn. At the same time, decrease center panel at regular intervals until it measures 7⅞ ins (20 cm) and 7 sts remain.

Pick up 20 sts evenly along neck edge and work a row of holes for cord as follows: *k1, yo, k2 tog*; now work ¾ in (2 cm) in single rib. Bind off.

Make a length of crocheted chain, using yarn double (1 strand each of 1st and 2nd colors), and thread through holes.

Bootees. Materials: 1 oz/29 gr of same yarn in first color; a small amount in second color; 1 pr of no 5 needles; 1 crochet hook size F/5; 2 small spare needles (optional).

Stitches used: garter stitch, single rib (see page 69), crocheted chain.

Beige and green sweater

Bonnet, bootees and mitts in 2 colors

Using main color, cast on 27 sts and work 2 ins (5 cm) in single rib. Work a row of holes for cord as follows: *k2, yo, k2 tog*. Work a further 2 rows in single rib, ending with a wrong side row. Leave first and last 9 sts on spare needles (or on a length of yarn) and work in garter stitch, using second color, on center 9 sts for 1½ ins (4 cm). Now, using main color, work in garter st across sts on left side, pick up 5 sts along left instep, work across the 9 center sts, pick up 5 sts along right instep and work across sts on right side (37 sts). Work a further / rows in garter st. Bind off. Make another bootee in exactly the same way.

To make up and complete: join backs of bootees and sew up seam along soles using a flat seam and very neat stitches. Using crochet hook and two strands of yarn (1 each in main and second color), work 2 lengths of chain and thread them through holes, to tie at centre front.

Mitts. Materials: ½ oz/15 gr yarn in first and second color; 1 pr of no 5 needles; 1 crochet hook size F/5.

Stitches used: garter stitch, single rib (see page 69), crocheted chain.

Using second color, cast on 14 sts and work 1½ ins (4 cm) in single rib. Change to garter st and work 4 rows in main color, 2 rows in second color, 2 rows in main color, 2 rows in second color and then, in main color, decrease over the next 6 rows until 1 stitch remains. Fasten off.

Make another mitt in exactly the same way.

Finishing: join side seams. Using crochet hook and two strands of yarn (1 each in main and second color), work 2 lengths of chain and thread them through between the end of single rib border and beginning of garter st on each mitt.

Blue and white bootees

Materials: 1 oz/29 gr of sport weight yarn in blue and a small amount of white; 1 pr of no 2 needles; 1 crochet hook size B/1; 2 small spare needles (optional).

Stitches used: stockinette stitch, garter stitch, single rib (see page 69). These bootees are started from the soles.

Using blue yarn, cast on 27 sts and work 9 rows in garter st, increasing 1 stitch on each side of central stitch on alternate rows. Change to white yarn and work 9 rows in st st, decreasing on the central stitch on every row.

Work a row of holes for cord as follows: *k2, k2 tog, yo*. Using blue yarn, work 9 rows in single rib. Bind off. Make a second bootee in exactly the same way.

Finishing: join backs of bootees and sew seam along soles as invisibly as possible. Using crochet hook and two strands of yarn (1 each in blue and white), work 2 lengths of chain and thread through holes so that they tie at center front.

Blue and white bootees and pink bootees

Pink and blue bootees and bib

Pink bootees

Materials: 1 oz/29 gr of fingering or baby yarn in pink; a length each of blue, red and green yarn; 1 pr of no 5 needles.

Stitches used: single rib (see page 69), stockinette stitch, garter stitch.

Cast on 40 sts and work 3½ ins (9 cm) in single rib. Now continue for 1⅛ ins (3 cm) in garter st and then for a further ¾ in (2 cm) in st st. Bind off.

Make a second bootee in exactly the same way.

Finishing: join sides of bootees with a flat seam. The lower part, worked in st st, should now be turned to the inside to form the sole. Embroider a small flower in blue yarn, with green leaves and a red center, on one side of each bootee (this will become the front). Make two lengths of looped cord (see page 56) and thread them through knitting about 2¾ ins (7 cm) down from top edges, so that they tie just above embroidered flowers. Turn single rib border down on each bootee so that its edge is on a line with cord.

Pink and blue bootees

Materials: 1 oz/29 gr no 5 cotton in pink and a small amount in dark blue; 1 pr of no 2 needles; 2 small spare needles (optional); 1 crochet hook size B/1.

Stitches used: garter stitch, stockinette stitch, single crochet, corded edge (see page 36).

Using pink cotton, cast on 30 sts and work 1½ ins (4 cm) in garter st. Work a row of holes for cord as follows: *k2, yo, k2 tog*. Leaving first 10 and last 11 sts on spare needles (or length of yarn), work ¾ in (2 cm) in st

209

Bootees with red and blue stripes

st on center 9 sts. At this stage, work heart motif, following diagram no 4 (see page 132), and then continue for another ¾ in (2 cm) in st st.

With left and right needles respectively, pick up the side sts of rectangle worked in st st (for instep) and work across all sts for 1⅛ ins (3 cm) in garter st. Bind off.

Make second bootee in exactly the same way.

Finishing: sew up the feet and then, using crochet hook and dark blue cotton, work a row of sc and a row of corded edge. Make 2 lengths of looped cord (see page 56), using cotton double (1 strand each of pink and blue), and thread them through holes to tie at center front.

Pink and blue bib

Materials: 1 oz/29 gr of no 5 cotton in pink and a small amount in dark blue; 1 pr of no 2 needles; 1 crochet hook size B/1.

Stitches used: garter stitch, stockinette stitch, single crochet, corded edge (see page 36).

Using pink cotton, cast on 40 sts and work ¾ ins (2 cm) in garter st. Continue for 6 rows in st st but working first and last 5 sts of every row in garter st. Now work 3 little hearts, in blue, following diagram no 4 on page 132 and retaining garter st border.

Work a further 2 ins (5 cm) in st st, still with garter st border, and then work child's initial based on sample letters in diagram no 5 on page 132.

After working another ¾ in (2 cm) in st st and garter st borders, as before, ending with a purl row, bind off 3 sts at beg of next row, k12, bind off center 10 sts, k15. Next row, bind off 3 sts, k12. *Work on these sts, for right tie, in garter st, decreasing another 4 sts at neck edge and 3 sts at shoulder edge on alternate rows. Continue on remaining 5 sts until tie measures 7 ins (18 cm). Bind off.*

Return to 12 sts at left side and work as for right tie from * to *.
Finishing: using blue cotton, work a row of sc and a row of corded edge all round bib.

Baby bootees with red and blue stripes

Materials: 1 oz/29 gr of sport weight yarn in main color; ½ oz/15 gr in red and a small amount in dark blue; 1 pr of no 2 needles; 2 small spare needles (optional); 1 crochet hook size B/1.

Stitches used: stockinette stitch and reversed stockinette st, twisted rib (see page 69), garter stitch, crocheted chain.

Using red yarn, cast on 40 sts and work in r st st for 4 rows. Now work 1 row in garter st, using dark blue yarn. Change to main color and work for 2 ins (5 cm) in twisted rib. Now work a row of holes for cord as

Bibs in 2 colors: left, primrose and brown; right, yellow and brown

follows: *k2, yo, k2 tog*. Leave 14 sts from each end of row on spare needles (or on a length of yarn) and continue on center 12 sts for 2 ins (5 cm) in st st. Using dark blue yarn, knit across 14 sts at left-hand side, pick up and knit 9 sts from edge of instep just worked, knit the 12 center sts, pick up and knit 9 sts from second edge of instep and then work across the 14 sts at right-hand side (58 sts).

Using red yarn, work 3 rows in r st st, then 6 rows in st st with main color and another 3 rows in r st st with red yarn.

Finish off the bootee with main color, working 1⅛ ins (3 cm) in st st and decreasing the center 14 sts on each row until 1 stitch remains. Fasten off.

Make a second bootee in exactly the same way.

Finishing: join back edges and sew seam along sole as invisibly as possible. Using crochet hook and 3 strands of yarn (1 strand each of main color, dark blue and red), make 2 crocheted chain cords and thread them through holes to tie at center front. Still with all 3 colors, make 4 small pompons and stitch them securely to cord ends.

Yellow and brown bib

Materials: 1 oz/29 gr of cotton yarn in yellow and a small amount in brown; 1 pr of no 6 needles; 1 crochet hook size G/6.

Stitches used: stockinette stitch, seed stitch (see page 76), single crochet, corded edge (see page 36), crocheted chain.

Using brown cotton, cast on 24 sts

and work 4 rows in seed st. Continue for 5⅛ ins (13 cm) in st st, changing color every 2 rows. Now bind off center 20 sts and work 1½ ins (4 cm) in st st, on each side separately, using brown cotton. Bind off.

Finishing: Using yellow cotton, work 1 row of sc and 1 row of corded edge all round bib. Using 1 strand of yellow and 1 of brown cotton, make 2 lengths of crocheted chain to tie round neck and attach one to each inside top corner of neck opening.

Bib in primrose and brown

Materials: 1 oz/29 gr of cotton yarn in primrose yellow and a small amount in brown; 1 pr of no 4 needles; 1 crochet hook size F/5.

Stitches used: garter stitch, stockinette stitch, single crochet, corded edge, crocheted chain.

Using main color, cast on 37 sts and work 4 rows in garter st. Continue in st st, working 4 sts in garter st at beg and end of each row, at the same time working a double dec (sl 1, k2 tog, psso) on center 3 sts of every knit row until 21 sts remain. Still in st st and retaining garter st border, increase 1 st on each side of central stitch on each plain row until there are 37 sts on needle again. Work 3 rows straight and then bind off center 13 sts and work on each side separately in st st with garter st border on outside edges for 6 rows. Bind off.

Now work a row of sc and a row of corded edge all round bib in brown cotton. Make 3 10 ins (25 cm) lengths of crocheted chain cord, using brown cotton, and sew one to each side of neck edge and tie the other in a bow, at center of bib.

Red and white coverlet

Materials: 2 skeins (3½ oz/100 gr) of worsted weight yarn in red and 1 in white; 1 pr of no 10½ needles; 1 crochet hook size I/9.

Stitches used: garter stitch, stockinette stitch, single crochet, corded edge (see page 36).

Using red yarn, cast on 72 sts and work 1½ ins (4 cm) in garter st. Now follow diagram no 14 (see page 134) until flower pattern has been completed and 5½ ins (14 cm) worked, with a border of 4 sts in garter st at beg and end of every row (18 cm). Still retaining garter st border, work a further 7 ins (18 cm) in st st.

Now follow diagram no 15 (see page 134) for another 2⅜ ins (6 cm) and then work 7 ins (18 cm) in st st.

Repeat floral design – diagram no 14 on page 134 – for a further 5½ ins (14 cm), finishing with 1½ ins (4 cm) in garter st. Bind off.

Finishing: using crochet hook and white yarn, work a row of sc and a row of corded edge all around coverlet.

Red and white coverlet

Mohair coverlet

White coverlet

Materials: 2 skeins (3½ oz/100 gr) of worsted weight yarn in white; 1 pr of no 9 needles.

Stitches used: seed stitch (see page 76), window stitch (see page 72). Cast on 78 sts and work 5 rows in seed st. Continue working for 27½ ins (70cm) in window st, keeping the first and lasts 5 sts of every row in seed st. Work a further 5 rows in seed st. Bind off.

White coverlet

Mohair coverlet

Materials: 4 skeins (3½ oz/100 gr) of mohair yarn in periwinkle blue and a small amount of white wool; 1 pr of no 9 needles; 1 crochet hook size I/9.

Stitches used: banded openwork stitch no 2 (see page 121), single crochet (see page 36).

Cast on 70 sts and work in banded openwork stitch no 2, for 24 ins (60 cm). Bind off loosely.

Finishing: using crochet hook and double yarn (1 strand of blue mohair and 1 of white), work a row of sc all around coverlet.

KNITTED ACCESSORIES

Gloves, socks, hats, bags, belts – just some of the types of accessories that can be knitted very successfully. Such things as these can express individuality and personal taste, emphasizing the main colors in an outfit or introducing striking contrasts. The color schemes used in the following basic patterns are merely suggestions; the possible variations are limitless.

Gray mittens with 2-color design

Materials: 1¾ oz (50 gr) of worsted weight yarn in gray, small amounts in red and white, 1 pr of no 6 needles, spare needle (optional).

Stitches used: double rib (see page 66); stockinette stitch.

Using gray yarn, cast on 32 sts and work 2⅛ ins (5.5 cm) in dbl rib. Work 2 rows in st st and then start increasing for thumb as follows: 1st row: k15, inc 1 stitch on 16th and 17th sts, k to end. Next and foll rows: k15, inc 1 stitch, k2 (4, 6, 8, 10), inc 1 stitch, k15. There will now be 12 sts in center of row for thumb shaping and work should measure 2 ins (5 cm) from commencement of increases. Leave first and last 16 sts on spare needle (or a piece of yarn) and continue on center 12 sts for 1¾ ins (4.5 cm). Bind off over next 3 rows. Fasten off.

Now work on the 32 sts left on spare needle, following diagram no 11 (see page 133) for 5½ ins (14 cm). Bind off over next 4 rows. Fasten off.

Work a second mitten in exactly the same way.

Finishing: join sides and thumb with a flat seam. Using a length of red yarn, embroider the 3rd row from end of ribbing in duplicate stitch (see page 58) and the 6th row with white yarn in the same way.

Beige gloves with 2-color design

Materials: 1¾ oz (50 gr) of fingering weight yarn in beige and small amounts in orange and green; 1 set of double-pointed no 5 needles; cable needle; stitch holder.

Stitches used: stockinette stitch, double rib (see page 66), small cable stitch (see page 93).

Using green yarn, cast on 36 sts (12 sts on each needle) and work 3 rounds in dbl rib. Change to orange yarn and work another 3 rounds then return to green yarn and work a further 3 rounds.

Now introduce beige yarn and work in small cable for 1½ ins (4 cm), working the cable twists over the 2 knit sts of the dbl rib (only 1 stitch will actually be twisted over the other) and working in purl over the 2 purl of dbl rib.

Continue for a further ¾ in (2 cm) in st st and then start to shape for thumb as follows: using the 2 central sts as a base, continue working in rounds but increasing 1 stitch within these 2 stitches on the first and last stitch, on alternate rows, until there are 16 stitches between original 2 central sts. Leave these 16 sts on stitch holder.

Continue on the rest of the sts, casting on 2 sts at thumb opening which will replace the 2 used to start the thumb shaping. Work 1½ ins (4 cm) in st st, then work fingers as follows:

1st finger: take 6 sts from back side of thumb opening and 5 from palm and cast on 2 sts on opposite side to thumb opening, dividing these 13 sts between the 3 working needles, and work in rounds for 2⅜ ins (6 cm). Now decrease regularly over next 4 rounds until 1 stitch remains. Fasten off.

2nd finger: take 5 sts from back and 4 sts from palm, plus another 2 sts from those previously cast on between 1st and 2nd fingers, cast on 2 opposite those 2, and work in rounds on these 13 sts for 2¾ ins (7 cm). Now decrease regularly over next 4 rounds until 1 stitch remains. Fasten off.

3rd finger: take 4 sts from back, 4 sts from palm, another 2 sts from those previously cast on and 2 newly cast on; work these 12 sts as for 2nd finger.

4th finger: take 4 sts from back and 4 sts from palm, plus another 2 from cast on sts of previous finger, and work in rounds on these 10 sts for 1¾ ins (4.5 cm). Now decrease regularly over next 3 rounds until 1 stitch remains. Fasten off.

Thumb: return to sts left on stitch holder and continue working in rounds for 2 ins (5 cm). Now decrease regularly over next 3 rounds

Gray mittens with 2-color design

Beige gloves and hat with 2-color design

until 1 stitch remains. Fasten off.
Work second glove to match.

Finishing: sew up the tip of each finger and thumb, where sts have been decreased, as neatly as possible. Embroider a design in duplicate stitch (see page 58), with contrasting yarns, on back of each glove.

Beige hat with 2-color design

Materials: 1¾ oz (50 gr) of fingering weight yarn in beige and small amount in green and orange; 1 set of double-pointed no 5 needles; 1 cable needle.

Stitches used: stockinette stitch, double rib (see page 66), small cable stitch (see page 93).

Using green yarn, cast on 96 sts (32 sts on each needle) and work 2 rounds in dbl rib. Change to orange yarn and work another 3 rounds, then return to green yarn and work a further 3 rounds.

Introduce beige yarn and work 1⅜ ins (3.5 cm) as follows: *p2, 2 sts in single cable* (instead of p2 k2).

Now turn work inside out so that reverse side of work is on the outside (to form turn-back on hat). Continue as follows: *p2, 2 sts in single cable, p2, k10*. Proceed in this way for 5½ ins (14 cm) then, on alternate rows, work first 2 and last 2 sts of knit panels together until 8 sts remain. Bind off.

Finishing: sew up the 8 bound-off sts neatly at top of hat.

Brown cap

Materials: 2 oz (60 gr) of tweed yarn in a brown mixture; 1 pr of no 5 needles; crochet hook size C/2.

Stitches used: garter stitch, stockinette stitch, single crochet (see page 36).

Cast on 74 sts and work 1⅜ ins (3.5 cm) in garter st. Now bind off first 6 sts of next row and work on remaining 68 sts for a further 2⅜ ins (6 cm) in st st. Begin decreasing, knitting 2 sts tog at regular intervals until 1 st remains. Fasten off.

Finishing: join seam from top of cap to beginning of garter stitch border.

Make a button by working a circle of a few rows of sc. Run a thread all around edge of crocheted circle and pull thread to gather edges of crochet together. Stitch button to little tab formed by cast off sts on border and tack to garter st border underneath.

Rust-colored hat

Materials: 1 skein (3½ oz/100 gr) of bulky weight yarn in rust; 1 pr of no 10½ needles.

Stitches used: k8, p8 rib, stockinette stitch, garter stitch.

Cast on 48 sts and work in k8, p8 rib for 3 rows. Now alternate pattern and work: p8 over k sts and k8 over p sts. Continue thus, alternating the pattern every 3 rows, until work measures 4⅜ ins (11 cm).

Now work 2 rows in st st and continue in garter st for 4¾ ins (12 cm). On next row, start decreasing by knitting 2 sts tog every 6 sts. On foll rows, continue decreasing over sts decreased in previous row, so that the stitches knitted together form straight lines, until 8 sts remain. Do not bind these sts off but break off yarn, allowing a considerable length, thread it through sts on needle, slip sts off needle and draw thread up so that top of hat is neatly pulled together. Secure with a few stitches and then use rest of thread to join edges with a flat seam (sewing from wrong side as far as border and then sewing from right side). Turn alternating border to outside of hat.

*Rust-colored scarf and
striped yellow scarf*

Rust-colored hat and brown cap

Rust-colored scarf

Materials: 12 oz (300 gr) of fingering weight yarn in rust; 1 pr of no 5 needles.
Stitch used: English rib (see page 66).
Cast on 60 sts and work 59 ins (150 cm). Bind off fairly loosely. Work a fringe (see page 55) about 4 ins (10 cm) deep at each end.

Striped yellow scarf

Materials: 4 skeins (1¾ oz/50 gr) of sport weight yarn in yellow and small amounts of green and brown; 1 pr of no 4 needles.
Stitches used: mock English rib (see page 67).
Using yellow yarn, cast on 74 sts and work 1½ ins (4 cm) in mock English rib. Still in mock English rib, work as

follows: 1 in (2.5 cm) with green yarn, 3/8 in (1 cm) with yellow, 1 in (2.5 cm) with green, 1 1/8 ins (3 cm) with yellow, 1 1/2 ins (4 cm) with brown, 3/8 in (1 cm) with yellow, 1 1/2 ins (4 cm) with brown, 1 3/4 ins (4.5 cm) with yellow, 3/4 in (2 cm) with green, 3/8 in (1 cm) with brown and 3/4 in (2 cm) with green.

Continue with yellow yarn for 45 ins (115 cm) and then repeat colored stripes, in reverse order. Bind off fairly loosely.

Finishing: work a fringe (see page 55) about 6 ins (15 cm) deep at both ends, using 2 strands of each color.

Shawl in shades of blue

Materials: 5 skeins (3 1/2 oz/100 gr) of fingering weight yarn in light blue and 2 sks in a blue mixture; 1 pr of no 4 needles; 1 crochet hook size G/6.

Stitches used: stockinette stitch, garter stitch, crocheted chain stitch, single crochet (see page 36).

Using the blue yarn, cast on 6 sts and work in st st for 15 ins (38 cm) increasing 1 st on each side of the center st, and 1 st at beg and end of row on every purl row (wrong side of work). In the same way, work a further 8 ins (20 cm) with the mixture yarn and then another 8 ins (20 cm) with the blue, ending with a purl row. Now work 1 row as follows: *k2 tog, yo, k3*. Work 2 rows in st st without increasing and then a second row of holes: *k3, yo k2 tog*. Work 2 more rows in st st and 2 rows in garter st.

Finishing: using crochet hook, work a row of sc along both lower edges. On return row, work 6 chain to turn, then 1 sc into 3rd sc, *ch5, 1 sc into 3rd sc* to end. Work a further 4 rows of loops as follows: ch7 to turn, 1 sc into 3rd ch of next loop, *ch5, 1 sc into 3rd ch of next loop*, alternating the yarn on each row so as to end with a blue row.

Work a row of sc on the other 2 sides.

Make a cord with 4 lengths of the blue mixture yarn and thread it through both rows of holes to give a slanting effect. Secure it firmly at each end on wrong side of shawl.

Black and Lurex shawl

Materials: approx 14 oz (350 gr) of wool and Lurex mixture; 1 pr of no 4 needles.

Stitches used: lacy stitch no 3 (see page 118).

Cast on 300 sts and work in lacy st no 3, decreasing 1 stitch at each end of every 1st and 3rd row of pattern (right side of work), until work measures 36 ins (90 cm).

Finishing: work a double knotted fringe (see page 56) about 10 ins (25 cm) deep along the 2 shorter sides.

Ribbon bag

Materials: approx 14 oz (350 gr) of narrow colored ribbon or tape; 1 pr of no 15 needles; lining.

Stitches used: mesh stitch no 1 (see page 119), garter stitch.

Cast on 16 sts and work 14 ins (36 cm) in mesh st no 1. Bind off. Work a second piece to match. Now cast on 4 sts and work a shoulder-strap 31 1/2 ins (80 cm) long in garter st. Bind off.

Finishing: join the 2 main pieces together on three sides, leaving one narrow end open. Attach shoulder-strap at each side. Sew lining, insert into bag and stitch neatly to bag around top edge.

Shawl in shades of blue

Black and Lurex shawl

Belt in woven stitch

Materials: 1 oz (29 gr) cotton string; 1 pr of no 4 needles; 1 crochet hook size C/3; 1 metal buckle.

Stitches used: woven stitch no 1 (see page 87), single crochet, corded edge (see page 36).

Cast on 10 sts and work 39½ ins (1 m) in woven st no 1. Bind off.

Finishing: using crochet hook, work 1 row of sc and 1 row of corded edge along all edges, to give a corded effect, and sew the buckle to one end as neatly as possible.

Bed jacket

Materials: 6 skeins (1¾ oz/50 gr) of sport weight yarn in a variety of colors; 1 pr of no 5 needles; 1

Belt in woven stitch

crochet hook size F/5.

Stitches used: garter stitch; mesh stitch no 1 (see page 119), single rib (see page 69), single crochet, corded edge (see page 36).

Cast on 70 sts and work 47 ins (120 cm) in mesh st no 1, working the first and last 4 sts of every row in garter st and changing yarn color every 2 rows.

Finishing: pick up all the sts along one end of the strip and, on 1st row, *k2 tog, p2 tog* to end of row. Now work in single rib for 2½ ins (6 cm). Bind off. Work wrist at opposite end to match.

Join wrist seams and with crochet

Ribbon bag

Bed jacket

Plain or fancy slippers

hook work 1 row of sc and 1 row of corded edge along both long edges.

Plain or fancy slippers

Materials: 3½ oz (100 gr) of sport weight yarn in turquoise; 1 set of double-pointed no 4 needles; 2 pieces of velvet.
Stitches used: stockinette stitch.
Cast on 100 sts (33, 33, 34) and work 2 rounds in st st. Start shaping for toe by decreasing 1 stitch on each side of center st, on alternate rows, 3 times. Continue for 2¾ in (7 cm) decreasing in the same way but every 4 rows. Bind off. Work a second slipper in the same way. Turn inside out, using purl as right side.
Finishing: cut 2 soles from the velvet (using an old slipper as a pattern), remembering to cut a right and left shape, as velvet is not reversible. Using a decorative stitch, join upper part of slipper to sole; make 2 pompons (see page 55) 3 ins (8 cm) in diameter and sew one to front of each slipper.
To make the slippers with colorful inserts, work in st st and introduce various colors, in single rows or in bands, as you wish. If there is a wide band of one color, embroider a few flowers or geometric designs to add an exotic touch. (Do not turn inside out.)

Striped socks

Materials: 1¾ oz (50 gr) of bulky yarn in each color: beige, green and white; small amounts in rust and brown; 1 set of double-pointed no 7 needles, 2 stitch holders.
Stitches used: single rib (see page 69), stockinette stitch.
Using brown yarn, cast on 40 sts (14, 14, 12). Work 2 rows in single rib. Change to rust colored yarn and work 4 rows. Change to beige yarn and work 2½ ins (6.5 cm). Continue in green yarn for ¾ in (2 cm), in white yarn for 1 in (2.5 cm) and in green yarn for a further 2¾ ins (7 cm), still in single rib.
Change to st st and work in white yarn for 1⅛ ins (3 cm), in rust for ¾ in (2 cm) and in white for 1⅛ ins (3 cm). Continue in green for 1⅛ ins (3 cm).
Shape for heel as follows: leaving the first 12 and last 13 sts on stitch holders, work 18 rows in st st on center 15 sts, purling first and last stitch of every knit row. At this point, put first and last 4 sts on spare needles and, working only on the 7

center sts, on every row incorporate 1 stitch from each side (i.e. at beg of every row on right side of work, knit last stitch from right side together with first of central stitches; at end of row, slip last of central stitches over first stitch on left-hand side).

To complete heel, use green yarn and pick up 9 sts – those purled on right side of the 18 rows in st st, and work in the round again, on 4 needles, decreasing 1 stitch 4 times every 2 rows on each side of the picked up stitches. After completion of heel, continue with green yarn for 2⅜ ins (6 cm). Now change to white and work 2⅜ ins (6 cm), then 2 rows in green and another 2⅜ ins (6 cm) in beige.

Start shaping for toe, having marked 2 sts the same distance apart on each side of foot with a colored thread, as follows: on every row, slip the stitch immediately to the left of marked stitch over next stitch and slip the stitch immediately to the right of marked stitch over next stitch until 1 st remains. Fasten off. Work second sock to match.

Striped socks

Long striped socks

Materials: 1¾ oz (50 gr) of bulky yarn in each color: beige, brown and rust; 1 set of double-pointed needles no 7. Stitches used: single rib (see page 69), stockinette stitch.

Using beige yarn, cast on 40 sts (12, 14, 14) by the tubular method and work 1 in (2.5 cm) in single rib. Still using beige yarn, continue for ⅜ in (1 cm) in st st and then work 2 ins (5 cm) in rust, gradually working 6 increases (46 sts). Now work 1 round using brown and rust alternately (k1 brown, k1 rust); next round, work in brown; next round, alternate colors as before. Work 1⅛ ins (3 cm) more in rust. Now work 1

Long striped socks

round using rust and beige alternately (k1 rust, k1 beige).

(Every change of color is preceded by a row worked in color just used alternating with color about to be used. As no further instructions are given for this interim row, it must be remembered each time a change of color is indicated.)

Continue in beige yarn for 2⅜ ins (6 cm), then in rust for ¾ in (2 cm) followed by brown for another 3½ ins (9 cm), decreasing 6 sts progressively at one side only (this will be back of sock). Now work 1 alternating row in rust and brown, 1 row in rust and another row in the same alternating colors.

Start heel shaping: using brown yarn, working only on the back 15 sts, leaving the other sts for the time being, work in st st on these 15 sts but purl first and last stitch of every knit row. When 18 rows have been completed, work only on the 5 center sts, picking up the first and last stitch from each side on every row (i.e. on each knit row, work last stitch from right side together with first of central stitches; at end of same row, slip last of central stitches over first stitch on left side).

To complete, pick up the 9 sts purled at each edge of knit side of the 18 rows worked in st st and work in the round again, on 4 needles, decreasing 1 stitch 4 times every 2 rows on each side of the picked-up stitches.

After completion of heel, work in rust yarn for 2⅜ ins (6 cm) and then in beige for 3⅛ ins (8 cm). Now work a row, alternating 1 st beige and 1 st rust, then a row in rust followed by another row alternating the same colors. Continue for ¾ in (2 cm) more in beige.

Start shaping for toe, having marked 2 sts the same distance apart on each side of foot, with a colored thread, as follows: on every row, slip the stitch immediately to the left of marked stitch over next stitch and slip the stitch immediately to the right of marked stitch over next stitch until 1 st remains. Fasten off. Work second sock to match.

Hat in blue, red and white

Materials: 1¾ oz (50 gr) of fingering yarn in dark blue; 1 oz (29 gr) of fingering yarn in white; ½ oz (15 gr) of fingering yarn in red; 1 set of double-pointed needles no 6.

Stitches used: single rib (see page 69), stockinette stitch.

Using dark blue yarn, cast on 80 sts (28, 28, 24) and work for 2¾ ins (7 cm) in single rib; then work 4 rows in st st. Now follow diagram no 10 on page 133 for 5⅛ ins (13 cm) without shaping, using all 3 colors.

Still following pattern from diagram, decrease for top by knitting 2 sts tog regularly over last 10 rows until 5 sts remain. Break off yarn, thread through remaining sts and close hole by pulling sts together. Fasten off securely.

To complete: make a pompon (see page 55) in dark blue yarn and stitch it firmly to top of hat. Turn ribbed border back.

Hat in blue, red and white

*Rust-colored mittens and
ear-hugging helmet*

Ear-hugging helmet

Materials: 1 oz (29 gr) each of sport weight yarn in rust, beige and orange; 1 pr of no 9 needles; 1 crochet hook size I/9, stitch holder or spare needle.

Stitches used: stockinette stitch, single crochet, corded edge (see page 36), crocheted chain stitch.

This helmet is worked in triple yarn (1 strand of each color), starting from one of the earflaps, as follows: cast on 3 sts and work 3 rows in st st, increasing 1 st at each end of all 3 rows. Now cast on another 6 sts on right side of earflap. Leave all these sts to one side (on a stitch holder or spare needle) and either break off all 3 strands or start another ball of each color. Cast on 3 sts for second earflap and work as 1st earflap except that the 6 sts must be cast on at left side. Now work across these 6 sts and across 2nd earflap, cast on 12 sts and work across 1st earflap together with its cast on sts.

Continue working on all 42 sts for 4 ins (10 cm). Shape top by working 2 together across all sts of next 2 rows. Break off yarn, thread through remaining sts and pull sts together. Fasten off securely.

Finishing: join back seam and, using crochet hook, work 1 row of sc and 1 row of corded edge all round edges of helmet. Make a pompon (see page 55) and 2 lengths of crocheted chain to tie under chin; sew pompon and ties securely into place.

Rust-colored mittens

Materials: 1 oz (29 gr) of sport weight yarn in rust; 1 pr of no 4 needles, stitch holder (optional).

Stitches used: stockinette stitch, single rib (see page 69).

Cast on 32 sts and work 1¾ ins (4.5 cm) in single rib. Continue for ¾ in (2 cm) in st st. Leave all except the 2 center sts on a spare needle (or slip onto a length of yarn). Working on the 2 sts, continue for 2 ins (5 cm), increasing 1 st at each side of central sts on every row until there are 12 sts. Continue straight for a further 1⅛ ins (3 cm). Work 2 sts tog over next 3 rows (1 st remains). Bind off, leaving a long enough strand to sew up side seam of thumb.

Rejoin yarn to remaining stitches and work 2 ins (5 cm) in st st. Work 2 sts tog over next 4 rows. Break off yarn, leaving a long enough strand to sew up side seams.

KNITTING FOR THE HOME

Knitting can be adapted in many ways to make those little extras that help to give individuality to any home. Afghans, cushion covers, bedspreads, scatter rugs, table mats, etc. may highlight a color scheme or introduce splashes of multi-color into an otherwise monotone décor. Textures, too, can vary between simple hard-wearing cotton worked in interesting stitches, through many blends of man-made fibers and wool, to gleaming satin and velvet ribbons.

Once again, the designs you will find here are merely basic ideas which your own imagination and skill can develop into really original, creative work.

Cable stitch cushion

Materials: 3 sks (3½ oz/100 gr) of bulky yarn in red; 1 pr of no 7 needles; 1 cushion pad about 16½×16½ ins (42×42 cm).
Stitches used: stockinette stitch, open cable stitch (see page 91).
Cast on 50 sts and work for 15¾ ins (40 cm) in open cable stitch.

Bind off.
For back of cushion, cast on 50 sts and work in st st until back measures same as front. (This may also be worked in open cable stitch, but a little more yarn may be needed.)
Finishing: with right sides of work together, join on 3 sides. Turn right side out, insert pad and join 4th seam.

Cable stitch cushion and patchwork cushion

Patchwork cushion

Materials: 6 sks (1¾ oz/50 gr) of sport weight yarn in a range of colors; 1 pr of no 2 needles; 1 cushion pad.

Stitch used: garter stitch.

Cast on 20 sts and work 2⅜ ins (6 cm) in garter st. Bind off.

This makes one square. Make as many as required to cover cushion pad all round.

Finishing: arrange the squares in the color sequence preferred, with the garter stitch ridges at right angles to each other. Sew squares together, using a neat flat seam, to form a bag with one side open. Insert pad and sew up 4th side neatly.

Bayadere cushion

Materials: 3 or 4 oz (100 gr) of yarn scraps will be required, in a variety of colors. The size of needles will depend upon the thickness of yarn used. 1 cushion pad and a square of velvet or similar fabric for cushion back (optional).

Stitches used: seed stitch (see page 76), stockinette stitch (if a fabric back is not used).

With first color, cast on 120 sts and work 4 rows in seed st. Rep 4 times, changing color every 4 rows and binding off 20 sts at beg of last row of 5th color.

Continue in the same way on these 100 sts, working 4 rows in each of another 5 colors and binding off 20 sts at beg of last row of 5th color band. Work same on 80, 60, 40 and 20 sts. Bind off.

To work second part, cast on 100 sts and work as before, reducing the number of sts progressively to 80, 60, 40 and 20.

If a fabric back is not used, with one color only, work a square in st st to same size as 2 pieces just completed.

Finishing: using a flat seam, join the 2 graduated pieces so that color blocks are at right angles to each other. Place fabric or knitted square, with wrong side outside, on multi-

Left, Bayadere cushion; right, rush-matting stitch cushion

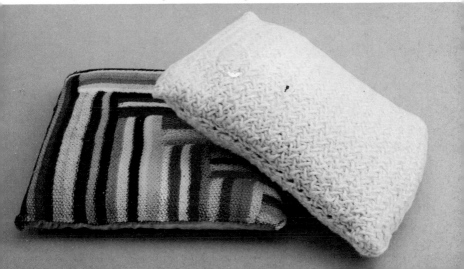

colored square and join on 3 sides. Turn right side out, insert pad and join fourth seam neatly.

Rush-matting stitch cushion

Materials: 3 sks (3½ oz/100 gr) of natural (Aran type) worsted wt yarn; 1 pr of no 9 needles; 1 cushion pad.
Stitch used: rush-matting stitch (see page 86).
Cast on 47 sts and work 17½ ins (44 cm) in rush-matting st. Bind off. Work a second piece to match.
Join the 2 pieces together on 3 sides. Turn right side out, insert cushion pad to fit and join 4th seam neatly.

Bed-cover in multi-colored triangles

Materials: 60 skeins (1¾ oz/50 gr) of sport weight yarn in a range of colors; 1 pr of no 5 needles; 1 crochet hook size F/5.
Stitches used: stockinette stitch, single crochet, corded edge (see page 36).
Each triangle is worked as follows: cast on 27 sts and work in st st, decreasing 1 stitch at beg of every row (1 dec on right side of work and 1 dec on wrong side) until 1 st remains. Fasten off.
Work as many triangles as required to give measurements of about 53 x 77 ins (135 x 196 cm).
Finishing: Arrange all the pieces in the color sequence desired and sew together, from wrong side, using a flat seam.

Using crochet hook and yarn in one color only, work a border 1½ ins (4 cm) deep all round bed-cover in single crochet, finishing off with 1 row of corded edge.

Double-bed coverlet in outlined multi-color squares

Materials: 120 skeins (1¾ oz/50 gm) of sport weight yarn in a range of colors; 1 pr of no 5 needles; 1 crochet hook size F/5.
Stitches used: seed stitch (see page 76), single crochet, crocheted chain stitch.
This coverlet is made up of 88 squares, arranged in 11 strips of 8 squares each. Each square is made as follows: cast on 55 sts and work about 8¼ ins (21 cm) in seed st (measure to ensure work is exactly square). Bind off. Count the number of rows and work all the other squares to same specification, to ensure uniformity.
Finishing: using crochet hook, work 1 row of single crochet in dark blue yarn (or whatever you decide to have as the outlining color) all round each square. Still using crochet hook, join all the squares together with outlining yarn by working through 2 edges together in single crochet. Now work 3 rows of single crochet around entire edge of coverlet and complete with a row of picots by working as follows: *ch 5, slip st into 3rd ch from hook, ch 2, skip 2 sts, 1 slip st into next st*.

Child's picture: night at sea

Materials: small amounts of bulky weight yarn in dark blue, off-white, yellow, red, and dark blue variegated; 1 pr of no 7 needles; 1 crochet hook size H/8.

Opposite, Bed-cover in multi-colored triangles

On following pages, Double-bed coverlet in outlined multi-color squares

Two children's pictures: left, night at sea; right, ginger cat

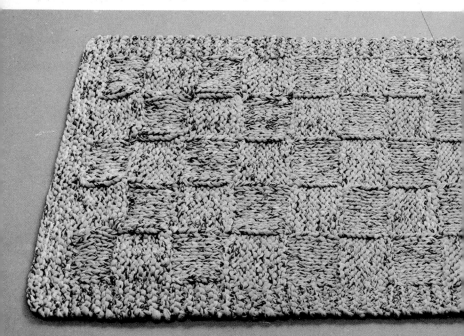

Stitches used: stockinette stitch; single crochet; corded edge (see page 36).

With dark blue variegated yarn, cast on 30 sts and work 2 ins (5 cm) in st st. Continue – following diagram no 8 (see page 132) – until work measures 8⅝ ins (22 cm). Bind off.

To complete: using crochet hook and off-white yarn, work 1 row of sc all around picture and then 1 row of corded edge.

Child's picture: ginger cat

Materials: 1 skein (3½ oz/100 gr) of bulky weight yarn in off-white and in reddish brown; small amounts of bulky weight yarn in red, dark brown, and yellow; 1 pr of no 7 needles; 1 crochet hook size H/8.

Stitches used: stockinette stitch, crocheted chain stitch, single

crochet, corded edge (see page 36).

Using off-white yarn, cast on 36 sts and work 1 in (2.5 cm) in st st. Continue, following diagram no 13 (see page 134) for 8¼ ins (21 cm), ending with a further 1 in (2.5 cm) in off-white. Bind off.

To complete: embroider the cat's eyes with yellow yarn, its nose with red yarn and, after making a few short lengths of crocheted chain in black yarn, sew whiskers in place.

Now, using crochet hook and dark brown yarn, work 2 rows of sc and 1 row of corded edge all around picture.

Scatter-rug in colored tape or ribbon

Materials: 35 oz of colored tape or ribbon; 1 pr of no 10 needles.

Stitches used: garter stitch, checkerboard stitch (see page 70) worked in blocks of 8 knit and 8 purl stitches. Cast on 50 sts and work 5 rows in garter st. Keeping the first and last 5 sts of every row in garter st, work 75 cm 29½ ins (75 cm) in checkerboard stitch, ending with a further 5 rows in garter st. Bind off.

Checker board rug

Materials: 44 oz of heavy loopy yarn in several colors; 1 pr of no 15 needles; 1 crochet hook size F/5.

Stitches used: garter stitch, single crochet (see page 36). This rug is made up of 5 strips consisting of 5 rectangles each. Each strip is made as follows: cast on stitches to a width of 8 ins (20 cm) and work about 13¾ ins (35 cm) in garter st, using the first color. (Each rectangle

Scatter-rug in colored tape or ribbon

will use about 1¾ oz/50 gr of yarn).
Change color and work another rectangle in the same way, continuing in this way until the 5 rectangles have been completed. Work 4 more strips, altering the order of the colors so that they form a diagonal pattern.
Finishing: join all the strips together with a flat seam, so that the stitches do not show on right side. In one color only, work 2 rows of sc around rug.

Square table centerpiece

The three patterns on the following pages are examples of what intricate knitted effects can be achieved. However their complexity is such that they should not be attempted until the techniques described in this book have been fully mastered. For the sake of conciseness the following system of abbreviation has been adopted:

r = knit stitch
a = slip one, knit one, pass slipped stitch over
g = knit 2 together as if to knit
v = 1 twisted knit stitch (worked through back of st)
e = purl stitch
3 = slip one, knit 2 together, pass slipped stitch over
(x) = 1 stitch crossed to the left
1 = yarn round needle
³ = 1 knit stitch worked twice (first into front of stitch and then into back of stitch)

If the abbreviation is accompanied by a figure and within brackets – for example, (3r) – this indicates the number of times the operation has to be repeated (the example given

Checker board rug

236

would therefore mean k3). Where 2, 3, 4 or 5 times is written out in full, all the instructions that follow it, or those in square brackets, should be repeated the prescribed number of times.

This type of work is worked in rounds on 4 or 5 needles. The instructions for each round correspond to one pattern repeat and should be repeated into remaining stitches.

Materials: 1½ oz/50 gr of cotton for lacework; 1 set of double-pointed needles no 00; 1 crochet hook size 00.

Using crochet hook, make a chain of 8 stitches and join with a slip stitch into first chain to form a circle. Divide these stitches between 3 needles. Continue as follows:

1st round: v 1 1 v

2nd round and all even numbered rounds: work exactly as previous round.

3rd round: v v 1 1 v v

5th round: v v 1 r r 1 v v

7th round: v v 1 (4r) 1 v v

9th round: v v 1 r g 1 1 a r 1 v v 1

11th round: v v 1 g 1 1 a g 1 1 a 1 v v 1 v v 1 v 1

13th round: (3r) 1 a g 1 1 a g 1 (3r) 1 r 1 v 1 r 1

15th round: a r r 1 3 3 1 r r g 1 (3r) 1 v 1 (3r) 1

17th round: a r r g r r g 1 (5r) 1 v 1 (5r) 1

19th round: a (3r) g 1 r 1 a r g 1 r 1 v 1 1 r 1 a r g 1 r 1

21st round: a r g (3r) 1 3 1 (3r) 1 v 1 (3r) 1 3 1 (3r) 1

23rd round: 1 3 1 (5r) 1 v 1 (5r) 1 3 1 (5r) 1 v 1 (5r)

24th round: work exactly as previous round.

Using crochet hook join the stitches into groups in the following order: 3 sts, 5 sts, 3 sts, 5 sts, 3 sts, 3 sts, 5 sts, 3 sts, 5 sts. Between each group of sts, work 10 chain stitches.

The stitches are now arranged on 4 needles to start working the border. The instructions after the asterisk * are only to be carried out at the end of each needle, to correspond with the corners of the table center.

1st round: (25r) * 1

2nd round and all even numbered rounds: work exactly as previous round.

3rd round: (25r) * 1 r 1

5th round: a (4r) 1 g 1 1 a g 1 1 a g 1 1 a 1 (4r) g v * 1 3 1

7th round: a (4r) 1 a g 1 1 a g 1 1 a g 1 (4r) g 1 v 1 * 1 3 1

9th round: a (4r) 1 3 g 1 1 a 3 1 (4r) g 1 r 1 v 1 r 1 * 1 r 1 v 1 r

11th round: a (4r) 1 3 3 1 (4r) g 1 (3r) v 1 (3r) 1 * 1 (3r) 1 v 1 (3r) 1

13th round: a (4r) g (4r) g 1 (5r) 1 v 1 (5r) 1 * 1 (5r) 1 v 1 (5r) 1

15th round: 3 (5r) 3 1 r 1 a r g 1 r 1 v 1 r 1 a r g 1 r 1 * 1 r 1 a r g 1 r 1 v 1 r 1 a r g 1 r 1

17th round: 3 r 3 1 (3r) 1 3 1 (3r) 1 v 1 (3r) 1 3 1 (3r) 1 * 1 3 1 ** (5r) 1 v 1 ** 7 times, (5r)

18th round: as previous round.

Using crochet hook, work stitches off together in groups of 3 and 5 working 10 chain stitches between each group.

Round table centerpiece

Materials: 1 oz/29 gr of cotton for lacework: 1 set of double-pointed needles no 00; 1 crochet hook no 00.

Start with 4 sts and work as follows:

1st round: 1 r

2nd round and all even numbered rounds: work exactly as previous round.

3rd round: 1 r r

5th round: r twice (1r)

7th round: r 4 times (1r)

9th round: a r 4 times (1r) g

11th round: a r r 5 times (1r) g

13th round: a (3r) 4 times (1g) 1 (3r) g

Square table centerpiece

15th round: a (4r) 5 times (1r) 1 (4r) g
17th round: 3 g (10r) (3g) 1
19th round: a (11r) g 1 r 1
21st round: a (9r) 1 (3r) 1
23rd round: a (7r) g 1 3 1 r 1
25th round: a (5r) g 1 (3r) 1 r 1 (3r) 1
27th round: a (3r) g 1 r 1, 3 times (1r) 1 r 1
29th round: a r g 1 (3r) 1 r 1 (3r) 1 r 1 (3r) 1
31st round: 3 1 r 5 times (1r) 1 r 1
33rd round: v 1 (3r) 1 (repeat over entire round)

34th round: work exactly as previous round.

Using crochet hook, work stitches off together in groups of 3, working 10 chain stitches between each group.

8-pointed table centerpiece

Materials: 3½ oz/100 gr of cotton for lacework; 1 set of double-pointed needles no 00; 1 crochet hook size 00.

Start with 2 sts and work as follows:
1st round: v 1
2nd round and all even numbered rounds: work exactly as previous round.
3rd round: v 1 r 1
5th round: v 1 r (x) 1
7th round: v 1 r (2x) 1
9th round: v 1 r (3x) 1
11th round: v 1 r (4x) 1
13th round: v 1 r (5x) 1
15th round: 1 v 1 r (6x) 1
17th round: 1 (3r) 1 a (x) r g a (2r) g
19th round: 1 (2r) 1 1 a r 1 a r g a g
21st round: 1 g 1 1 a g 1 1 a 3 g
23rd round: 1 (3r) g 1 1 a (3r) 1 g
25th round: 1 (2r) g 1 1 a g 1 1 a (2r) 1 v

27th round: 1 r g 1 1 a g 1 1 a g 1 1 a (2r)
29th round: g 1 1 a g 1 1 a g 1 1 a g 1 1 a
31st round: 1 a g 1 1 a g 1 1 a g 1 1 a g 1
33rd round: g 1 1 a g 1 1 a g 1 1 a g 1 1 a 1
35th round: 1 a g 1 1 a (2r) 1 r 1 (2r) g 1 1 a g 1
37th round: g 1 1 a g 1 1 g 1 (3r) 1 a 1 1 a g 1 1 a
39th round: 1 a g 1 1 a g 1 (5r) 1 a g 1 a g 1
41st round: g 1 1 a r g 1 r 1 a r g 1 r 1 1 a g 1 1 a
43rd round: 1 a (2r) g 1 (3r) 1 3 1 (3r) 1 a r r g 1

Round table centerpiece

240

8-pointed table centerpiece

45th round: g 1 1 3 1 (5r) 1 v 1 (5r) 1 3 1 1 a

47th round: 1 a g 1 r 1 a r g 1 3 1 a 3 g 1 r 1 a g 1

49th round: r g 1 (3r) 1 3 1 (3r) 1 3 1 (3r) 1 a r

51st round: g 1 (5r) 1 v 1 (5r) 1 v 1 (5r) 1 a

53rd round: transfer 1 stitch from left to right and work: 1 r 1 a r g 1 r 1 a r g 1 3 1 a r g 1 r 1 g

55th round: 1 (3r), 3 times [1 3 1 (3r)], 1 v

57th round: (5r), 3 times [1 v 1 (5r)], 1 ^{3} 1

59th round: a r g, 3 times [1 (3r) 1 a r g], 1 (x) v 1 (x) 1

61st round: 3 1, 3 times [(5r), 1 3 1], (2x) 1 v 1 (2x) 1

63rd round: twice [1 a r g (3r)], 1 g r g

1 g 1 (3x) 1 v 1 (3x) 1

65th round: a, 3 times [1 3 1 (5r)], 1 g
1 (4x) 1 v 1 (4x) 1

67th round: a 1 a 1 a r g 1 (3r) 1 a r g 1
g 1 g 1 (5x) 1 v 1 (5x)] 1

69th round: a 1 a 1 3 1 (5r) 1 3 1 g 1 g
1 (6x) 1 v 1, 6 times 1

71st round: a, 3 times (1 a), r g, 3
times (1 g), 1 (7x) 1 v 1 (7x) 1

73rd round: a 1 a 1 a 1 3 1 g 1 g 1 g 1
(8x) 1 v 1 (8x) 1

75th round: a 1 a r g 1 g 1 g 1 (9x) 1 v
1 (9x) 1

77th round: a 1 a 1 3 1 g 1 g 1 g 1 (10x) 1
v 1 (10x) 1

79th round: a 1 a r g 1 g 1 (11x) 1 v 1
(11x) 1

81st round: a 1 3 1 g 1 (12x) 1 v 1

(12x) 1

82nd round: work exactly as previous round.

Using crochet hook, work sts off together in the following order: (5 sts tog) 5 times, (3 sts tog) once, (5 sts tog) 5 times, and so on for entire round, separating each group of sts with 12 chain sts.

If you are already experienced in this type of work, you will be able to make this table centrepiece into a tablecloth by increasing the number of center rounds (as far as the 51st) and then continuing as from the 53rd round to complete the tablecloth with the point motif, which will remain unchanged.

Traycloth/placemat

Traycloth/placemat in cotton mixture

Traycloth/placemat

Materials: 1¾ oz/50 gr of knitting cotton in ecru; 1 oz/29 gr of knitting cotton in dark blue; 1 pr of no 4 needles; 1 crochet hook size E/4.

Stitches used: garter stitch, stockinette stitch, single crochet, corded edge (see page 36).

Using ecru cotton, cast on 76 sts and work 4 rows in garter st. Continue in st st, following diagram no 12 (see page 133) for 8⅝ ins (22 cm). Now work a further 4 rows in garter st and bind off.

Finishing: using crochet hook and dark blue cotton, work 1 row of sc and 1 row of corded edge along all 4 sides.

Traycloth/placemat in cotton mixture

Materials: 3½ oz/100 gr of knitting cotton mixture (4 strands used together); a small amount of knitting cotton in white; 1 pr of no 5 needles; 1 crochet hook size F/5.

Stitches used: ladder stitch (see page 121), single crochet (see page 36), picot edging (see page 36) corded edge (see page 36).

Cast on 50 sts and work nearly 12 ins (30 cm) in ladder st. Bind off.

Finishing: using crochet hook and cotton mixture, work 3 rows of sc along all 4 sides; change to white cotton and work another row in sc and 1 row in corded edge.

USEFUL AND FUN THINGS TO KNIT WITH SCRAPS

In these last few pages you will find a wide range of small things that are easy to make. Some are useful (such as the pot-holders and saucepan mats for the kitchen) and others are simply for fun (like the toys and little doll for the children). They represent just a few ways in which scraps of yarn may be used up and you will probably be able to think of lots more ideas of your own.

Pot-holder – a face

Materials: small quantities of pink and blue knitting cotton; a little light brown crochet cotton no 5; 1 pr of no 4 needles; 1 crochet hook size E/4.
Stitches used: garter stitch, single crochet, corded edge (see page 36).
Using pink cotton, cast on 4 sts and work 1 row in garter st (wrong side of work). Increase 1 stitch at each end of next and every alternate row until there are 24 sts on needle. Continue straight for a further 2 ins (5 cm). Bind off. Using blue cotton, cast on 30 sts and work 1 row in garter st. Decrease 1 stitch at each end of next and every alternate row until 1 stitch remains. Fasten off.
Finishing: using crochet hook and blue cotton, work 1 row of sc and 1 row of corded edge all round edge of hat; with pink cotton, work in same way round edge of face.
Place wide edge of hat over wide edge of face and stitch together with very neat stitches, from the wrong side.
Embroider the mouth and eyes in light brown cotton.
Make a loop by casting on 16 sts in blue cotton; knit 1 row. Bind off. Fold in half and stitch firmly to top of hat.

Pot-holder – a house

Materials: small quantities of no 5 cotton in green and rust; 1 pr of no 4 needles; 1 crochet hook size E/4.
Stitches used: garter stitch, single crochet, corded edge (see page 36).
Using green cotton, cast on 32 sts and work 3½ ins (9 cm) in garter st. Change to rust-colored cotton and decrease 1 stitch at each end of every alternate row (right side of work) until 10 sts remain. Bind off.
Make 2 windows by casting on 8 sts in rust-colored cotton and working 1⅛ ins (3 cm). Bind off. Work second window to match. Make door by casting on 8 sts in rust-colored cotton and working 2⅛ ins (5.5 cm).
To complete: sew windows and door in position with small invisible stitches. Work 1 row of sc and 1 row

Some ideas for pot-holders

of corded edge in green cotton along green edges and work in same way, using rust-colored cotton, along edges of roof.

Make a loop by casting on 16 sts in rust-colored cotton and knitting 1 row. Bind off. Fold in half and stitch neatly, at back of work, to one side of roof.

Pot-holder in horizontal Tunisian stitch

Materials: 1½ oz/50 gr of no 5 cotton, used double, in a flecked shade; a small amount of no 5 cotton in dark brown; 1 pr of no 6 needles; 1 crochet hook size F/5.
Stitches used: horizontal Tunisian stitch (see page 95), single crochet, corded edge (see page 36).

Using 2 strands of flecked cotton, cast on 20 sts and work 4¾ ins (12 cm) in horizontal Tunisian stitch. Bind off.
To complete: using dark brown cotton and crochet hook, work 1 row of sc and 1 row of corded edge along all 4 sides. Make a loop by crocheting a short length of chain with dark brown cotton and working 1 row of sc. Fold in half and attach firmly to one corner.

Pot-holder in strips of colored cloth or tape

Materials: 1½ oz/50 gr of strips of cloth, tape or ribbon; 1 pr of no 10 needles; 1 crochet hook size H/8.
Stitches used: woven stitch no 1 (see page 87), single crochet (see

page 36).
Cast on 12 sts and work in woven stitch no 1 until a square is obtained. Bind off.
Using crochet hook, work 1 row of sc along all 4 edges. Make a loop and stitch firmly to one corner.

Saucepan mat in strips of colored cloth or tape

Materials: approx 7 oz/200 gr of strips of colored cloth or tape; 1 pr of no 10 needles; 1 crochet hook size H/8.
Stitches used: woven stitch no 1 (see page 87), single crochet, corded edge (see page 36).
Cast on 10 sts and work in woven stitch no 1 until a square is obtained. Bind off. Work a second square in the same color. Work 2 more squares in a contrasting color.
Join all 4 squares neatly together

and, using crochet hook, work 1 row of sc and 1 row of corded edge along all 4 sides of the large square thus made. Make a loop and attach firmly to one corner.

Pot-holder in ecru and light blue

Materials: 1 oz/29 gr of cotton in 2 colors (worked double); 1 pr of no 9 needles; 1 crochet hook size H/8.
Stitches used: stockinette stitch, single crochet, corded edge (see page 36).
Cast on 25 sts and work in st st, making a double dec (slip one, k2 tog, psso) on center 3 sts on every knit row (right side of work) until 1 stitch remains. Fasten off.
To complete: using crochet hook, work 1 row of sc and 1 row of corded edge all around pot-holder. Make a short length of crocheted chain for loop, work 1 row in sc; fold in half and stitch firmly to top of pot-holder.

Saucepan mat in ecru and light blue

Materials: 1½ oz/50 gr each of cotton in light blue and ecru; 1 pr of no 9 needles; 1 crochet hook size H/8.
Stitches used: stockinette stitch, single crochet, corded edge (see page 36).
This saucepan mat is made in 6 sections, 3 in light blue and 3 in ecru, each of which is made as follows: (cotton is worked double throughout) cast on 25 sts and work in st st, making a double dec (slip 1, k2 tog, psso) on center 3 sts of each row, until 1 stitch remains. Fasten off.
To complete: when the 6 sections have been made, join them together – in alternating colors – with dupli-

Pot-holder and saucepan mat in colored ribbon

246

Saucepan mat (left) and pot-holder in ecru and blue

cate stitch. Using crochet hook and 1 strand of both colors, work 1 row in sc and 1 row in corded edge all round outside edge.

Dachshund draft stopper

Materials: 1¾ oz/50 gr of sport weight yarn in brown; same amount in yellow; 1 oz (29 gr) of sport weight yarn in beige; a small piece of white felt and one of blue felt; 1 pr of no 4 needles; 1 crochet hook size E/4; stuffing (old, clean nylon panty hose with the waistband cut off are ideal for this).

Stitches used: stockinette stitch, garter stitch, single crochet (see page 36).

Using brown yarn, cast on 56 sts and work about ¾ in (2 cm) in st st, continue with beige yarn for ⅜ in (1 cm) and for ⅛ in (½ cm) with yellow yarn.

Continue for a further 24 ins (60 cm), alternating the colors in the same way. Work another 6 ins (15 cm) with brown yarn. Now start decreasing by working 2 sts tog for 2 ins (5 cm) until 1 stitch remains. Fasten off. Join face seam on wrong side, turn

right side out and insert stuffing, sewing up body as you go with a flat seam. With brown yarn, pick up stitches at open end and work 2 ins (5 cm), decreasing all stitches as before.

Ears: using 2 strands of yellow yarn, cast on 15 sts and work 13¾ins (35cm) in garter st. Bind off. Work 1 row of sc, in brown yarn, all round. Sew this strip in position, over top of head, gathering it slightly in the middle to give the impression of ears.

Nose: make a pompon with yellow yarn about 1½ ins (4 cm) in diameter and attach it to front of face with small stitches.

Paws: using 2 strands of yellow yarn, cast on 10 sts and work 2 ins (5 cm) in garter st. Bind off. Work 3 more pieces exactly the same. Sew all 4 paws neatly in position.

Tail: using 2 strands of yellow yarn, cast on 15 sts and work 4 ins (10 cm) in garter st. Bind off. Sew up one end and join sides. Stuff and stitch into position.

Eyes: cut 2 oval shapes from white felt and 2 smaller ones from blue felt. Sew the blue shapes on to the white and stitch into position.

Pink mouse

Materials: 1 oz/29 gr of fingering or baby yarn in pink and a small amount in gray; 1 pr of no 6 needles; 2 small round black buttons.
Stitch used: garter stitch.
Using pink yarn, make a pompon about 3–3½ ins (8 cm) in diameter. Make a short length of looped cord (see page 56) with gray yarn for tail. The ears consist of 2 gray triangles and 2 pink triangles, made as follows: cast on 8 sts and work in st st, decreasing 1 stitch at each end of every knit row until 1 stitch remains. Fasten off.
Finishing: sew each gray triangle onto a pink triangle and sew the 2 ears into position on the pompon. Cut a little of the pompon away, in front of the ears, to give the impression of a little pointed face. Sew the 2 buttons onto the face as eyes and stitch the tail firmly in place.

Multi-colored caterpillar

Materials: small amounts of worsted weight yarn in red, white, crimson, light brown, brick red, blue and yellow; 2 black buttons.
Make 1 pompon in each color and join them together in a line, making sure that the colors are well arranged. Sew the 2 buttons for eyes at each side of the first pompon which will be the head.

Dachshund draft stopper

Multi-colored caterpillar and pink mouse

Doll

Materials: 1 oz/29 gr of worsted weight yarn in light blue and small amounts of brown, pink, pale pink, dark blue, fuchsia and scarlet; 1 pr of no 9 needles; some scraps of cotton (or nylons) for stuffing.

Stitches used: garter stitch, stockinette stitch.

Using light blue yarn, cast on 25 sts for the skirt and work 3½ ins (9 cm) in garter st. Continue for 2 rows in st st, knitting 2 sts tog for entire length of 1st row and purling next row normally (13 sts).

Continue with fuchsia yarn for another 6 rows in garter st. Change to dark blue yarn and repeat the 2 rows of st st (decreasing on 1st row, as before). Continue with pink yarn, increasing 1 stitch at each end of every row until there are 20 sts on needle. On next 3 rows, work 2 sts tog until 1 st remains. Fasten off.

Finishing: join back. Pick up 5 sts from each side of last fuchsia row with fuchsia red yarn and work 10 rows in garter st. Cast off. Tie up the ends of these extensions to form the arms.

Doll

Stuff with scraps of cotton (or cut-up nylons). Embroider the eyes with brown yarn and the mouth with red yarn. Make a small fringe (see page 55) and sew to head, plaiting the lengths of yarn at each side of head and stitching them into place. Tie a little bow at end of both plaits.

249

Glasses case in turquoise cotton

Materials: 1 oz/29 gr of no 5 cotton in turquoise (worked double); 1 pr of no 4 needles; 1 crochet hook size E/4.

Stitches used: garter stitch, stockinette stitch, reversed stockinette stitch, twisted cable stitch (see page 91), single crochet, corded edge (see page 36).

Cast on 24 sts and work 12 rows in garter st. Now work pattern as follows: 8 sts in st st, 2 sts in reverse st st, 4 sts in twisted cable, 2 sts in reverse st st, 8 sts in st st. Continue in this way for 11 ins (28 cm), ending with another 12 rows in garter st.

Finishing: fold the strip in half and join long edges by crocheting them together in sc, work 1 row of corded edge over the sc.

Glasses cases: in Lurex and turquoise cotton

Glasses case in Lurex

Materials: 1 oz/29 gr of gold 'Lurex'; 1 pr of no 2 needles; 1 crochet hook size C/2.

Stitches used: garter stitch, mesh stitch no 1 (see page 119), single crochet, corded edge (see page 36). This case is made in one piece.

Cast on 12 sts and work 10 rows in garter st. Continue for 11 ins (28 cm) in mesh st no 1. Now work another 10 rows in garter st and cast off.

Finishing: fold the strip in half and join both long edges by crocheting them together in sc; work 1 row of corded edge over the sc.

Work 1 row of sc and 1 row of corded edge all round edge of open end.

INDEX

ace of spades stitch 115, *116*
armholes 45
asterisk 13

bag, ribbon 220, *223*
bed-cover in multi-colored triangles *230*, 231
bed jacket 222-4 *223*
belt in woven stitch 222, *223*
bibs
    pink and blue *209*, 210
    primrose and brown *211*, 212
    yellow and brown 211-12, *211*
binding off 50-51
blocking 56-8
bobbins 13
bolero in mock marabou 162-3, *162*
bonnet in two colors 206, *207*
bootees
    blue and white 208, *208*
    pink *208*, 209
    pink and blue 209-10, *209*
    with red and blue stripes 210-11, *210*
    in two colors 206-7, *207*
    white *199*, 200-201
    white and blue 202, *203*
    white and pink *197*, 198
borders 34-6
butterfly stitch 107, *107*
buttonholes 40-41, *40*

cable stitch
    alternating 91, *91*
    open 91-2, *91*
    plaited 92, *93*
    single 92-3, *93*
    small 93, *93*
    three-stitch 92, *92*
    twisted *90*, 91
    see also crossing stitches
cap, brown 218, *219*

cardigan, white zip-front 182-3, *183*
casting on
    double 19
    four needles 20-21
    normal method (crossed casting) 18-19
    thumb method 18
    tubular method 21-2
    two needles 19-20
caterpillar, multi-colored 248, *249*
centerpieces
    eight-pointed 239-42, *241*
    round 238-9, *240*
    square 236, 238, *239*
chain link stitch 62-3, *62*
checkerboard stitch 70, *71*
cherry stitch 63, *63*
    sloping 63, *63*
coats
    cream 178-9, *178*
    light brown 138, *139*, 140-41
    white 195-7, *196*
corded edge 36, *36*
cords 56
corners 38-9, *38*, *39*
coverlets
    double-bed 231, *232-3*
    mohair 215, *215*
    red and white 212, *213*
    white *214*, 215
crochet hooks 8, 12
cross-stitch 58
crossing stitches 26-7
cushions
    Bayadere 229-30, *229*
    cable-stitch 228, *228*
    patchwork *228*, 229
    rush-matting stitch *229*, 231

darts
    horizontal 50
    vertical 49-50

decreasing 13, 27, 30-33, *31-3*
diagonal stitch 82, *83*
diamond stitch
   embossed 83, *83*
   ridged 82, *82*
dividing knitting 52
doll 249, *249*
draft stopper 247, *248*
dress, yellow 192, *192*
dropped shoulder line 46
dropped stitches 13, 51
duplicate stitch 58

eightsome stitch 61, *61*
elongating a stitch 27

fan stitch
   no.1 129, *129*
   no.2 130, *130*
fancy stitch
   no.1 104, *104*
   no.2 104, *105*
   no.3 104, *105*
   no.4 105, *105*
   no.5 106, *106*
   no.6 106-7, *106*
finishing 58
floret stitch 72-3, *72*
flower stitch
   no.1 73, *73*
   no.2 73-4, *74*
   no.3 74-5, *75*
fringes 55-6

garter stitch 14, 24-5, *24*, 34, 35, *35*
Gaston's stitch 75, *75*
gauge 13
glasses cases
   in Lurex 250, *250*
   in turquoise cotton 250, *250*
gloves, beige 216-17, *217*
grafting 58
grill stitch 76, *76*

harebell stitch 100, *101*
hats
   beige *217*, 218
   blue, red and white 226, *226*
   rust-colored 218, *219*
helmets
   baby's *199*, 200
   ear-hugging 227, *227*

hems
   cat's tooth 37-8, *37*
   simple 37, *37*
herringbone stitch 86, *86*
honeycomb stitch 78-9, *79*

increasing 13, 28, *29*, 30, *30*

jackets
   evening 166, *167*
   light brown (child's) 186-7, *186*
   light brown (lady's) 144-5, *144*
   navy blue *140*, 141
   olive green 169-70, *170*
   red 179-80, *179*
   red tie-neck 187-8, *187*
   white 142, *143*
   white (child's) 180-81 *181*
   white with hood 145-6, *147*
jacquard designs 131-5
jerkins
   white hooded 188-9, *189*
   white outlined in brown 184, *184*

knit stitch
   basic 23
   in row below 27
   twisted 24
knit up 14
knitting, history of 7-10
knitting bags 13
knitting machines 8, 10
knitting needle cases 12
knitting needles 7-8, 10-12, 17

lacy stitch
   no.1 117, *118*
   no.2 (Trinity) 117, *118*
   no.3 118, *118*
   no.4 118, *119*
ladder stitch 121, *121*
large chain stitch 77, *77*
large diamond panel stitch 80, *81*
leaf stitch
   no.1 108-9, *109*
   no.2 110, *110*
   no.3 111, *111*
   no.4 111-12, *112*
lozenge stitch
   plain 77-8, *78*
   reversed 78, *78*

mesh stitch
  no.1 119, *119*
  no.2 119, *119*
  no.3 119, *120*
  no.4 120, *120*
  small 81, *82*
mittens
  gray 216, *217*
  rust-colored 227, *227*
mitts
  in two colors 207, *207*
  white and blue 202, *203*
mock polka-dot stitch 107, *107*
mosque stitch 113, *114*
moss stitch *see* seed stitch
mouse, pink 248, *249*
mullion stitch
  alternating 64, *64*
  open 101, *101*
  reversed 64, *65*

necklines
  mock turtle or turtle 45, *45*
  round 43-4, *44*
  square 44
  V 44, *45*

olive stitch 79, *79*
open flowery stitch 108, *108*
openwork stitches
  banded no.1 120, *121*
  banded no.2 121, *121*
  braided 126, *127*
  checkerboard *122*, 123
  diagonal 126, *126*
  lozenge 123-4, *123*
  nest 114-115, *115*
  plaited *124*, 125
  segments 122, *122*
  squared 124, *124*
  triangular 126-7 *127*
  V 125, *125*
  vertical no.1 *96*, 97
  vertical no.2 *96*, 97
overalls
  blue 193, *193*
  white, for baby 202-4, *205*
overcoat, off-white 136, *137*, 138

pants
  baby's brown *199*, 200
  baby's white and blue 201-2, *203*

parentheses 14
pass slipped stitch over 14, 27
pick up *see* knit up
picked-up stitches 34-5, *35*
picot edge 36, *36*
pictures
  cat *234*, 235
  night at sea 231, *234*, 235
pine-cone stitch 116, *117*
placemats *242*, 243
  in cotton mixture 243, *243*
pleats
  box 49, *49*
  imitation or sun-ray 49, *49*
  inverted 48-9, *48*
pockets
  incorporated 41, *42*, 43
  patch 41, *41*
  tailored 43
point protectors 12
pompons 55
poncho 164, *165*
position of hands and needles 16-17
posy stitch 112-13, *113*
pot-holders
  in colored strips 245-6, *246*
  in ecru and light blue 246, *247*
  with face design 244, *245*
  in horizontal Tunisian stitch 245, *245*
  with house design 244-5, *245*
pram outfits
  four-piece 201-2, *203*
  with squirrel motif 198-201, *199*
pullovers
  blue 152-3, *152*
  light blue sleeveless 194, *194*
  mauve 149-50, *149*
  red with V-neck 185-6, *185*
  white 170-72, *171*
purl stitch 23-4
  twisted 24
purse, evening *168*, 169

repairing knitting 52-4
repeat 14
reverse single crochet stitch *see* corded edge
rib stitches
  alternating 65, *65*
  alternating English *66*, 67
  with alternating florets 103, *103*

broad and narrow 70, *71*
  diagonal 70, *70*
  double 66, *66*
  English 66-7, *66*
  mock English 67, *67*
  openwork 103, *103*
  reverse 69, *69*
  rush-mat *65*, 66
  single 35, *35*, 69, *69*
  sloping *67*, 68
  Sylvia's *69*, 70
  twisted *68*, 69
  wavy 68, *68*
  wide 67, *67*
  see also under woven stitches
row 14
row counters 12
rug, checkerboard 235-6, *236-7*
  see also scatter rug
rush-matting stitch 86, *87*
  large 87, *87*

sail stitch 128, *128*
saucepan mats
  in colored strips 246, *246*
  in ecru and light blue 246-7, *247*
scarves
  rust-colored 219, *219*
  striped yellow 219-20, *219*
scatter-rug *234-5*, 235
seed stitch 35, 76, *76*
  double 76, *76*
segments stitch
  crossed 83, *84*
  horizontal 84, *85*
selvedges 14, 34, *34*
sewing up 58
shawls
  black and Lurex 220, *222*
  in shades of blue 220, *221*
shell stitch 102, *102*
skirts
  red *190*, 191
  striped, in mohair 163-4, *163*
  white, with shoulder straps 191,
    191
sleeves
  kimono 46-7
  raglan 45-6, *46*
  yoke 47, *47*
slip stitch 14, 27
slipover

red sleeveless (lady's) 177, *177*
  red sleeveless (man's) 161-2, *161*
slippers, plain or fancy 224, *224*
smocking stitch 84-5, *85*
socks
  long striped 225-6, *225*
  striped 224-5, *225*
stitch 14
stitch counters 12
stitch holders 12
stockinette stitch 14, *24*, 25, 58, 131
  on the bias 60, *60*
  reversed 25
  twisted 60, *61*
sweaters
  baby's 198-200, *199*
  beige and green 204-5, *206*
  blue 175-6, *175*
  blue polo-neck 146-8, *148*
  brown 155-6, *155*
  brown and beige 158-9, *158*
  gray 173-5, *174*
  hooded 150-52, *151*
  pink 154, *154*
  plaid/striped 156-7, *157*
  three-color 189-91, *190*
  tweed 159-60, *159*
  white and cerise *160*, 161
  white and gray 172-3, *173*
  white and pink 197-8, *197*
Swiss darning *see* duplicate stitch

tape measure 12, 13
tassels 54
tension 12, 13, 17, 131
through back loop 14
top, baby's 201, *203*
traycloth *242*, 243
  in cotton mixture 243, *243*
tree stitch 97, *97*
triangle stitch 94, *94*
Trinity stitch *see under* lacy stitch
trousers
  green 182, *182*
  light brown 181-2, *183*
tubular stitch 21-3, 36
Tunisian stitches
  horizontal *94*, 95
  sloping *94*, 95
turban stitch 90, *90*
two-piece, evening 166, 168-9, *168*